STEP INTO THE
CHINESE EMPIRE

Philip Steele

Consultant: Jessie Lim

southwater

This edition is published by Southwater,
an imprint of Anness Publishing Ltd, Hermes House,
88–89 Blackfriars Road, London SE1 8HA;
tel. 020 7401 2077; fax 020 7633 9499

www.southwaterbooks.com; www.annesspublishing.com

Anness Publishing has a new picture agency outlet for images for
publishing, promotions or advertising. Please visit our website
www.practicalpictures.com for more information.

UK agent: The Manning Partnership Ltd; tel. 01225 478444;
fax 01225 478440; sales@manning-partnership.co.uk
UK distributor: Grantham Book Services Ltd; tel. 01476 541080;
fax 01476 541061; orders@gbs.tbs-ltd.co.uk
North American agent/distributor: National Book Network;
tel. 301 459 3366; fax 301 429 5746; www.nbnbooks.com
Australian agent/distributor: Pan Macmillan Australia; tel. 1300 135 113;
fax 1300 135 103; customer.service@macmillan.com.au
New Zealand agent/distributor: David Bateman Ltd;
tel. (09) 415 7664; fax (09) 415 8892

Publisher: Joanna Lorenz
Managing Editor, Children's Books: Sue Grabham
Senior Editor: Neil Kelly
Project Editor: Sophie Warne
Editor: Charlotte Hurdman
Readers: Felicity Forster, Joy Wotton
Designers: Matthew Cook, Alison Walker
Illustration: Robert Ashby, Stuart Carter, Shane Marsh
Photography: John Freeman
Stylist: Konica Shankar
Additional Styling: Melanie Williams
Production Controller: Ann Childers

© Anness Publishing Ltd 1998, 2008

Anness Publishing would like to thank the following children for
modelling for this book: Lucilla Braune, Aileen Greiner, Francesca Hill,
Alex Lindblom-Smith, Sophie Lindblom-Smith, Daniel Ofori, Vanessa
Ofori, Edward Parker, Claudia Martins Silva, Clleon Smith, Nicky
Stafford, Saif Uddowlla, Kirsty Wells. Gratitude also to their parents, and
to Hampden Gurney and Walnut Tree Walk Schools.

ETHICAL TRADING POLICY
Because of our ongoing ecological investment program, you, as our
customer, can have the pleasure and reassurance of knowing that a tree is
being cultivated on your behalf to naturally replace the materials used to
make the book you are holding. For further information about this
scheme, go to www.annesspublishing.com/trees

PICTURE CREDITS
b=bottom, t=top, c=center, l=left, r=right
Ancient Art and Architecture Collection Ltd: pages 15br, 56tl, 58cl;
Bridgeman Art Library: pages 15tl, 16cl, 21tr, 23br, 25bl, 31tl, 31cl,
33bl, 41bl, 45tl, 46cl, 47cl, 47cr; Bruce Coleman: pages 25br, 39tl; James
Davis Worldwide Photographic Travel Library: pages 5tr, 17cl, 36br; C M
Dixon: pages 12tl, 14bl, 24tl, 30tr, 43tl, 44tr; E T Archive: pages 8l, 9tl,
9tr, 9bl, 11t, 11bl, 12bl, 15tr, 15bl, 17tr, 20br, 21br, 22tr, 22bl, 23bl,
24br, 25tr, 26tr, 27tr, 32bl, 40br, 43tr, 47tl, 49cl, 50cr, 54bl, 57cl, 61t;
Mary Evans Picture Library: pages 11br, 12br, 22br, 29tl, 42br,
59tl;FLPA: pages 43cr, 43br; Werner Forman Archive: pages 10bl, 13tr,
26cr, 29tr, 29cl, 38tr, 39bl, 39br, 40bl, 44cl, 48c, 50tl, 51cl, 55tr, 59tr;
Michael Holford: pages 4tl, 35tl, 35cl, 36tr, 37br, 41c, 58tr; The
Hutchinson Library: pages 52cl, 60c, 61cl; MacQuitty Collection:
pages 5c, 20tl, 21bl, 25tl, 27cl, 32tr, 37b, 41br, 43bl, 45tl, 46tl,
48tr, 53tl, 53tr, 53cl, 54tl, 55cl, 55br, 59cl; Papilio
Photographic: page 30cl; TRIP: pages 10br, 60tr; Visual Arts
Library: pages 8r, 9br, 14tl, 14c, 20bl, 23tr, 28cl, 34tl, 35cl,
40tl, 41tl, 41tr, 44cr, 49tl, 51tl, 51tr, 55tl, 56cl; ZEFA: pages 4c,
10tl, 13tl, 13b, 16tl, 18tr, 33tl, 33bl, 36bl, 37tl, 37tr, 38tl, 39tr,
47tr.

CONTENTS

An Ancient Civilization.......... 4

The Middle Kingdom............. 6

Makers of History.................... 8

The Sons of Heaven.................... 10

Religions and Beliefs................... 12

Chinese Society............................ 14

Towns and Cities.......................... 16

Houses and Gardens............................. 18

Home Comforts...................................... 20

Family Life.. 22

Farming and Crops................................. 24

Fine Food... 26

Markets and Trade.................................. 28

Medicine and Science............................. 30

Feats of Engineering..... 32

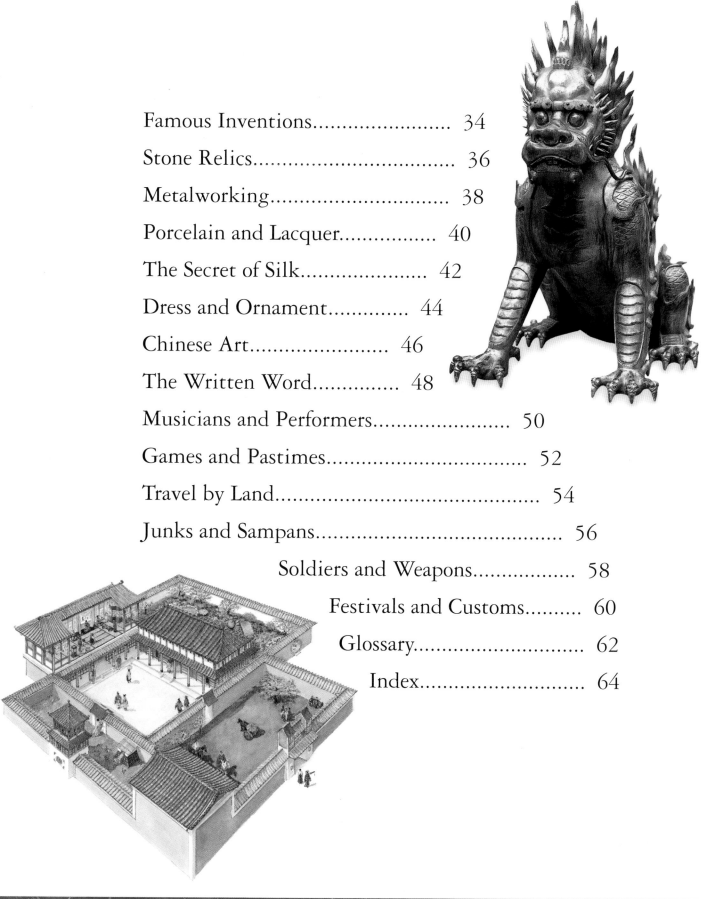

Famous Inventions...................... 34

Stone Relics.................................. 36

Metalworking............................. 38

Porcelain and Lacquer................ 40

The Secret of Silk...................... 42

Dress and Ornament............. 44

Chinese Art........................ 46

The Written Word.............. 48

Musicians and Performers...................... 50

Games and Pastimes................................ 52

Travel by Land.. 54

Junks and Sampans... 56

Soldiers and Weapons................. 58

Festivals and Customs......... 60

Glossary............................ 62

Index............................ 64

An Ancient Civilization

IMAGINE YOU COULD travel back in time 5,000 years and visit the lands of the Far East. In northern China you would come across smoky settlements of small thatched huts. You might see villagers fishing in rivers, sowing millet or firing pottery. From these small beginnings, China developed into an amazing civilization. Its towns grew into huge cities, with palaces and temples. Many Chinese became great writers, thinkers, artists, builders and inventors. China was first united under the rule of a single emperor in 221 B.C., and continued to be ruled by emperors until 1912.

China today is a modern country. Its ancient past has to be pieced together by archaeologists and historians. They dig up ancient tombs and settlements, and study textiles, ancient books and pottery. Their job is made easier because historical records were kept. These provide much information about the long history of Chinese civilization.

REST IN PEACE
A demon is trampled into defeat by a guardian spirit. Statues like this were commonly put in tombs to protect the dead from evil spirits.

ALL THE EMPEROR'S MEN
A vast model army marches again. It was dug up by archaeologists in 1974, and is now on display near Xian. The lifesize figures are made of terra-cotta (baked clay). They were buried in 210 B.C. near the tomb of Qin Shi Huangdi, the first emperor of all China. He believed that they would protect him from evil spirits after he died.

TIMELINE 7000 B.C.–110 B.C.

Prehistoric remains of human ancestors dating back to 600,000 B.C. have been found in China's Shaanxi province.
The beginnings of Chinese civilization may be seen in the farming villages of the late Stone Age (8000 B.C.–2500 B.C.). As organized states developed, the Chinese became skilled at working metals, making elaborate pottery and fine silk and at warfare.

*c.*7000 B.C. Bands of hunters and fishermen roam freely around the river valleys of China. They use simple stone tools and weapons.

Banpo hut

*c.*3200 B.C. Farming villages such as Banpo produce pottery in the thousands. The people typify the Yangshao culture.

*c.*2100 B.C. The legendary XIA DYNASTY (period of rule) begins its 400-year-reign.

*c.*2000 B.C. Black pottery is made by the people of the Longshan culture.

Shang bronze vessel

*c.*1600 B.C. Beginning of the SHANG DYNASTY. Bronze worked and silk produced. The first picture-writing is used (on bones for telling fortunes).

1122 B.C. Zhou ruler Wu defeats Shang emperor. Wu becomes emperor of the WESTERN ZHOU DYNASTY.

Zhou spearheads

7000 B.C.   2100 B.C.   1600 B.C.

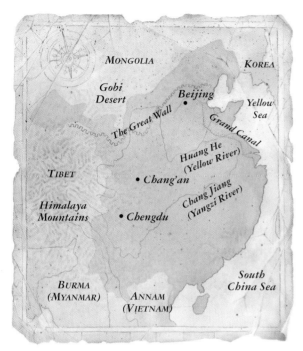

A Heavenly Hall

The Hall of Prayer for Good Harvest (*shown right*) is part of Tiantan, the Temple of Heavenly Peace in Beijing. It was originally built in 1420, but had to be rebuilt in the 1890s after it was destroyed by lightning. Buildings like this tell us about traditional technology and design, as well as about Chinese religious beliefs.

The Han Empire (206 B.C.–A.D. 220)

China grew rapidly during the Han dynasty. By A.D. 2 it had expanded to take in North Korea, the southeast coast, the southwest as far as Vietnam and large areas of Central Asia. Northern borders were defended by the Great Wall.

The Jade Prince

In 1968, Chinese archaeologists excavated the tomb of Prince Liu Sheng. His remains were encased in a jade suit when he died in about 100 B.C. Over 2,400 pieces of this precious stone were joined with gold wire. It was believed that jade would preserve the body.

Zhou soldier

771 B.C. Capital city moves from Anyang to Luoyang. Beginning of EASTERN ZHOU DYNASTY.

c.604 B.C. The legendary Laozi, founder of Daoism is born.

551 B.C. Teacher and philosopher Kong Fuzi (Confucius) is born.

513 B.C. Iron-working develops.

453 B.C. Break-up of central rule. Small states fight each other for 200 years. Work begins on the Grand Canal and the Great Wall.

221 B.C. China unites as a centralized empire under Zheng (Qin Shi Huangdi). The Great Wall is extended.

213 B.C. Qin Shi Huangdi burns all books that are not "practical."

Chinese writing

210 B.C. Death of Qin Shi Huangdi. The Terra-cotta army guards his tomb, near Chang'an (modern Xian).

206 B.C. QIN DYNASTY is overthrown. Beginnings of HAN DYNASTY as Xiang Yu and Liu Bang fight for control of the Han Kingdom.

202 B.C. The WESTERN HAN DYNASTY formally begins. It is led by a former official named Liu Bang, who becomes Emperor Gaozu.

200 B.C. Chang'an becomes the capital city of the Chinese empire.

terra-cotta warrior and horse

112 B.C. Trade with the people of Western Asia and Europe begins to flourish along the Silk Road.

| 780 B.C. | 550 B.C. | 210 B.C. | 140 B.C. | 110 B.C. |

The Middle Kingdom

CHINA IS A VAST COUNTRY, about the size of Europe. Its fertile plains and river valleys are surrounded by many deserts, mountains and oceans. The ancient Chinese named their land Zhongguo, the Middle Kingdom, and believed that it was at the center of the civilized world. Most Chinese are descended from a people called the Han, but the country is also inhabited by 50 or more different groups of people, some of whom have played an important part in Chinese history. These groups include the Hui, Zhuang, Dai, Yao, Miao, Tibetans, Manchus and Mongols.

The very first Chinese civilizations grew up around the Huang He (Yellow River), where the fertile soil supported farming villages and then towns and cities. These became the centers of rival kingdoms. Between 1700 B.C. and 256 B.C. Chinese rule spread southward to the Chang Jiang (Yangzi River), the great river of Central China. All of eastern China was united within a single empire for the first time during Qin rule (221–206 B.C.).

The rulers of the Han dynasty (206 B.C.–A.D. 220) then expanded the empire southward as far as Annam (Vietnam). The Chinese empire was now even larger than the Roman empire, dominating Central and Southeast Asia. The Mongols, from lands to the north of China, ruled the empire from 1279 to 1368. They were succeeded by the Manchu in 1644. In later centuries, China became increasingly inward-looking and unable to resist interference from European powers. The empire finally collapsed, with China officially declaring itself a republic in 1912.

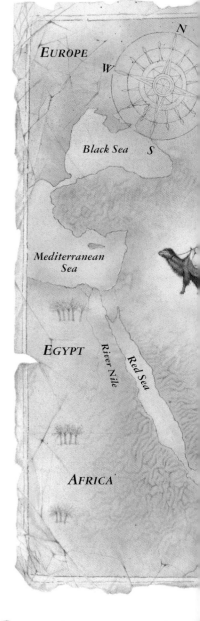

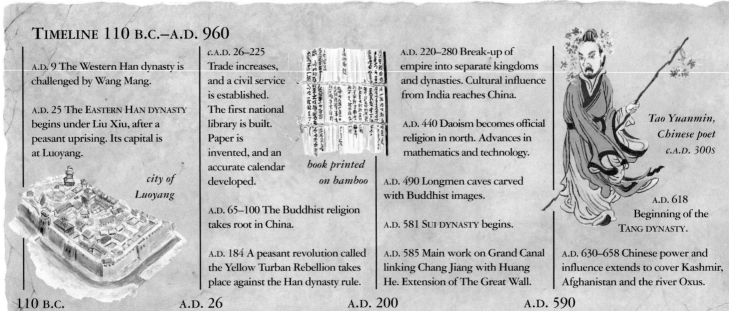

TIMELINE 110 B.C.–A.D. 960

A.D. 9 The Western Han dynasty is challenged by Wang Mang.

A.D. 25 The EASTERN HAN DYNASTY begins under Liu Xiu, after a peasant uprising. Its capital is at Luoyang.

city of Luoyang

c.A.D. 26–225 Trade increases, and a civil service is established. The first national library is built. Paper is invented, and an accurate calendar developed.

book printed on bamboo

A.D. 65–100 The Buddhist religion takes root in China.

A.D. 184 A peasant revolution called the Yellow Turban Rebellion takes place against the Han dynasty rule.

A.D. 220–280 Break-up of empire into separate kingdoms and dynasties. Cultural influence from India reaches China.

A.D. 440 Daoism becomes official religion in north. Advances in mathematics and technology.

A.D. 490 Longmen caves carved with Buddhist images.

A.D. 581 SUI DYNASTY begins.

A.D. 585 Main work on Grand Canal linking Chang Jiang with Huang He. Extension of The Great Wall.

Tao Yuanmin, Chinese poet c.A.D. 300s

A.D. 618 Beginning of the TANG DYNASTY.

A.D. 630–658 Chinese power and influence extends to cover Kashmir, Afghanistan and the river Oxus.

110 B.C.　　　　A.D. 26　　　　A.D. 200　　　　A.D. 590

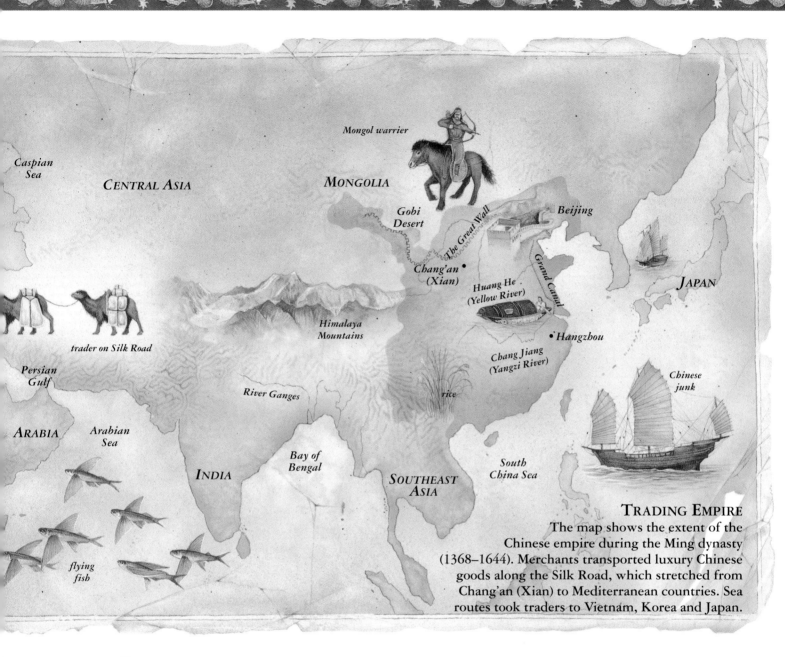

Mongol warrier

Caspian
Sea

CENTRAL ASIA

MONGOLIA

Gobi
Desert

Beijing

The Great Wall

Chang'an
(Xian)

Huang He
(Yellow River)

Grand Canal

JAPAN

Himalaya
Mountains

trader on Silk Road

Hangzhou

Persian
Gulf

Chang Jiang
(Yangzi River)

Chinese
junk

River Ganges

rice

ARABIA

Arabian
Sea

INDIA

Bay of
Bengal

SOUTHEAST
ASIA

South
China Sea

flying
fish

TRADING EMPIRE

The map shows the extent of the
Chinese empire during the Ming dynasty
(1368–1644). Merchants transported luxury Chinese
goods along the Silk Road, which stretched from
Chang'an (Xian) to Mediterranean countries. Sea
routes took traders to Vietnam, Korea and Japan.

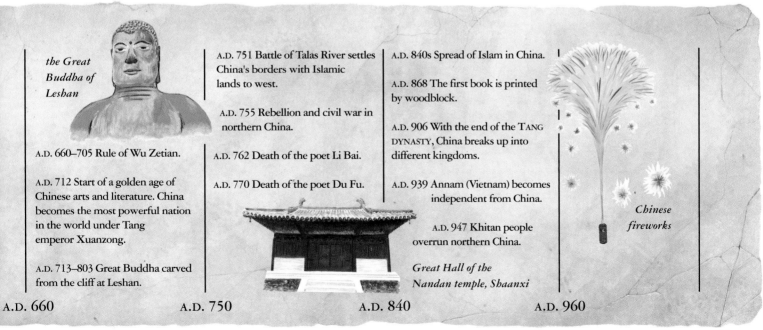

*the Great
Buddha of
Leshan*

A.D. 660–705 Rule of Wu Zetian.

A.D. 712 Start of a golden age of
Chinese arts and literature. China
becomes the most powerful nation
in the world under Tang
emperor Xuanzong.

A.D. 713–803 Great Buddha carved
from the cliff at Leshan.

A.D. 751 Battle of Talas River settles
China's borders with Islamic
lands to west.

A.D. 755 Rebellion and civil war in
northern China.

A.D. 762 Death of the poet Li Bai.

A.D. 770 Death of the poet Du Fu.

*Great Hall of the
Nandan temple, Shaanxi*

A.D. 840s Spread of Islam in China.

A.D. 868 The first book is printed
by woodblock.

A.D. 906 With the end of the TANG
DYNASTY, China breaks up into
different kingdoms.

A.D. 939 Annam (Vietnam) becomes
independent from China.

A.D. 947 Khitan people
overrun northern China.

*Chinese
fireworks*

A.D. 660   A.D. 750   A.D. 840   A.D. 960

Makers of History

GREAT EMPIRES ARE made by ordinary people as much as by their rulers. The Chinese empire could not have been built without the millions of peasants who planted crops, built defensive walls and dug canals. The names of these people are largely forgotten, except for those who led uprisings and revolts against their rulers. The inventors, thinkers, artists, poets and writers of imperial China are better known. They had a great effect on the society they lived in, and left behind ideas, works of art and inventions that still influence people today.

The royal court was made up of thousands of officials, astronomers, artists, craftsmen and servants. Some had great political power. China's rulers came from many different backgrounds and peoples. Many emperors were ruthless former warlords who were hungry for power. Others are remembered as scholars or artists. Some women also achieved great political influence, openly or from behind the scenes.

LAOZI (born *c.*604 B.C.)
The legendary Laozi is said to have been a scholar who worked as a court librarian. It is thought that he wrote the book known as the *Daodejing*. He believed people should live in harmony with nature, and his ideas later formed the basis of Daoism.

KONG FUZI (551–479 B.C.)
Kong Fuzi is better known in the West by the Latin version of his name, Confucius. He was a public official who became an influential teacher and thinker. His views on family life, society, and the treatment of others greatly influenced later generations.

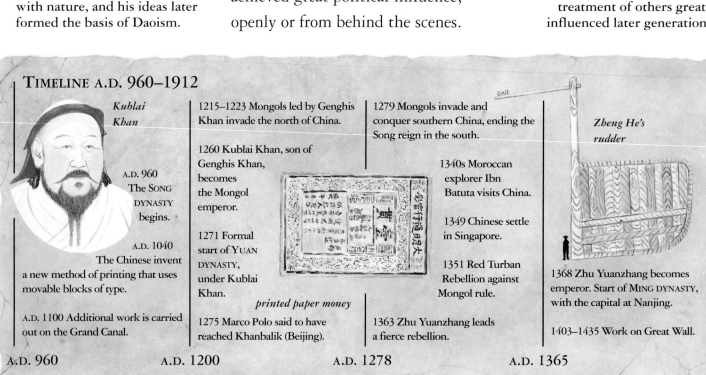

TIMELINE A.D. 960–1912

Kublai Khan

A.D. 960 The SONG DYNASTY begins.

A.D. 1040 The Chinese invent a new method of printing that uses movable blocks of type.

A.D. 1100 Additional work is carried out on the Grand Canal.

1215–1223 Mongols led by Genghis Khan invade the north of China.

1260 Kublai Khan, son of Genghis Khan, becomes the Mongol emperor.

1271 Formal start of YUAN DYNASTY, under Kublai Khan.

printed paper money

1275 Marco Polo said to have reached Khanbalik (Beijing).

1279 Mongols invade and conquer southern China, ending the Song reign in the south.

1340s Moroccan explorer Ibn Batuta visits China.

1349 Chinese settle in Singapore.

1351 Red Turban Rebellion against Mongol rule.

1363 Zhu Yuanzhang leads a fierce rebellion.

Zheng He's rudder

1368 Zhu Yuanzhang becomes emperor. Start of MING DYNASTY, with the capital at Nanjing.

1403–1435 Work on Great Wall.

A.D. 960   A.D. 1200   A.D. 1278   A.D. 1365

QIN SHI HUANGDI (256–210 B.C.)
Scholars beg for their lives before the first emperor. Zheng came to the throne of a state called Qin at the age of nine. He went on to rule all China and was given his full title, meaning First Emperor of Qin. His brutal methods included burying his opponents alive.

HAN GAOZU (256–195 B.C.)
In the Qin dynasty (221–206 B.C.) Liu Bang was a minor public official in charge of a relay station for royal messengers. He watched as the centralized Qin empire fell apart. In 206 B.C. he declared himself ruler of the Han kingdom. In 202 B.C. he defeated his opponent, Xiang Yu, and founded the Han dynasty. As Emperor Gaozu, he tried to unite China without using Qin's harsh methods.

EMPRESS WU ZETIAN
(AD624–705)
The Emperor Tang Gaozong enraged officials when he replaced his legal wife with Wu, his concubine (secondary wife). After the emperor suffered a stroke in A.D. 660, Wu took control of the country. In A.D. 690 she became the only woman in history to declare herself empress of China.

KUBLAI KHAN (A.D. 1214–1294)
The Venetian explorer Marco Polo visits Emperor Kublai Khan at Khanbalik (Beijing). Kublai Khan was a Mongol who conquered northern, and later southern, China.

1405–33 Chinese voyages of exploration under Zheng He.

1421 Bejing becomes the capital city of the Chinese empire.

Manchu warrior

1428 The Chinese are expelled from Annam (Vietnam).

1550 Japanese pirates mount raids on China. Mongols invade north again.

1644 Li Zicheng leads a rebellion against Ming rule. Manchu invasion. QING DYNASTY founded.

Boxer rebels

1673 Rebellions against Qing rule in south.

1839–42 First Opium War, as Britain forces China to accept opium imports from India.

1842 Treaty of Nanjing. Britain acquires Hong Kong.

1850–64 Taiping rebellion.

1858 Treaty of Tianjin. Chinese ports taken over by foreign powers.

1862 The Empress Dowager Cixi becomes regent.

1894–95 War with Japan. Loss of Taiwan.

1899–1900 Boxer Rebellion against Qing and foreign governments.

1908 Last emperor, Puyi, ascends to throne as a small boy.

1912 Declaration of republic by Sun Yatsen. Emperor Puyi abdicates.

Puyi, the last emperor

A.D. 1405   A.D. 1425   A.D. 1650   A.D. 1880   A.D. 1912

The Sons of Heaven

THE FIRST CHINESE RULERS lived about 4,000 years ago. This early dynasty (period of rule) was known as the Xia. We know little about the Xia rulers, because this period of Chinese history has become confused with ancient myths and legends. Excavations have told us more about the Shang dynasty rulers of over 3,000 years ago, who were waited on by slaves and had fabulous treasures.

During the next period of rule, the Zhou dynasty, an idea arose that the Chinese rulers were Sons of Heaven, placed on the throne by the will of the gods. After China became a powerful, united empire in 221 B.C., this idea helped keep the emperors in power. Rule of the empire was passed down from father to son. Anyone who seized the throne by force had to show that the overthrown ruler had offended the gods. Earthquakes and natural disasters were often interpreted as signs of the gods' displeasure.

Chinese emperors were among the most powerful rulers in history. Emperors of China's last dynasty, the Qing (1644–1912), lived in luxurious palaces that were cut off from the world. When they traveled through the streets, the common people had to stay indoors.

WHERE EMPERORS PRAYED
These beautifully decorated pillars can be seen inside the Hall of Prayer for Good Harvests at Tiantan in Beijing. An emperor was a religious leader as well as a political ruler, and would arrive here in a great procession each New Year. The evening would be spent praying to the gods for a plentiful harvest in the coming year.

TO THE HOLY MOUNTAIN
This stele (inscribed stone) is located on the summit of China's holiest mountain, Taishan, in Shandong province. To the ancient Chinese, Taishan was the home of the gods. For over 2,000 years the emperors climbed the carved steps to the temple to offer prayers.

IN THE FORBIDDEN CITY
The vast Imperial Palace in Beijing is best described as "a city within a city." It was built between 1407 and 1420 by hundreds of thousands of laborers under the command of Emperor Yongle. Behind its high, red walls and moats were 800 beautiful halls and temples, set amongst gardens, courtyards and bridges. No fewer than 24 emperors lived here in incredible luxury, set apart from their subjects. The Imperial Palace was also known as the Forbidden City, as ordinary Chinese people were not even allowed to approach its gates.

"WE POSSESS ALL THINGS"

This was the message sent from Emperor Qianlong to the British King George III in 1793. Here the emperor is being presented with a gift of fine horses from the Kyrgyz people of Central Asia. By the late 1800s, Chinese rule took in Mongolia, Tibet and Central Asia. All kinds of fabulous gifts were sent to the emperor from every corner of the empire, as everyone wanted to win his favor.

RITUALS AND CEREMONIES

During the Qing dynasty, an emperor's duties included many long ceremonies and official receptions. Here in Beijing's Forbidden City, a long carpet leads to the ruler's throne. Officials in silk robes line the steps and terraces, holding their banners and ceremonial umbrellas high. Courtiers kneel and bow before the emperor. Behavior at the royal court was monitored in great detail. Rules decreed what kinds of clothes could be worn and in what colors.

CARRIED BY HAND

The first Chinese emperor, Qin Shi Huangdi, is carried to a monastery high in the mountains in the 200s B.C. He rides in a litter (a type of chair) that is carried on his servants' shoulders. Emperors always traveled with a large following of guards and courtiers.

Religions and Beliefs

"THREE TEACHINGS FLOW INTO ONE" is an old saying in China. The three teachings are Daoism, Confucianism and Buddhism. In China they gradually mingled together over the ages.

The first Chinese peoples believed in various gods and goddesses of nature and in spirits and demons. The spirit of nature and the flow of life inspired the writings that are said to be the work of Laozi (born c.604 B.C.). His ideas formed the basis of the Daoist religion. The teachings of Kong Fuzi (Confucius) come from the same period of history but they stress the importance of social order and respect for ancestors as a source of happiness. At this time another great religious teacher, the Buddha, was preaching in India. Within 500 years Buddhist teachings had reached China, and by the Tang dynasty (A.D. 618–906) Buddhism was the most popular religion. Islam arrived at this time, and won followers in the northwest. Christianity also came into China from Persia, but few Chinese were converted to this religion until the 1900s.

THE MERCIFUL GODDESS
Guanyin was the goddess of mercy and the bringer of children. She was a holy figure for all Chinese Buddhists.

DAOISM—A RELIGION OF HARMONY
A young boy is taught the Daoist belief in the harmony of nature. Daoists believe that the natural world is in a state of balance between two forces—yin and yang. Yin is dark, cool and feminine, while yang is light, hot and masculine. The two forces are combined in the black and white symbol on the scroll.

A NEW FAITH—CONFUCIANISM
Kong Fuzi (Confucius) looks out at an ordered world. He taught that the well-being of society depends on duty and respect. Children should obey their parents and wives should obey their husbands. The people should obey their rulers, and rulers should respect the gods. All of the emperors followed the teachings of Confucianism.

CHINESE BUDDHA

Chinese monks carved huge statues of the Buddha from rock. Some can be seen at the Mogao caves near Dunhuang, where temples were built as early as A.D. 366. The Buddha taught that suffering is caused by our love of material things. Buddhists believe that we are born over and over again until we learn to conquer this desire.

ISLAM IN CHINA

This is part of the Great Mosque in Xian (ancient Chang'an), built in the Chinese style. The mosque was founded in A.D. 742, but most of the buildings in use today date from the Ming dynasty (1368–1644). Islam first took root in China in about A.D. 700. Muslim traders from Central Asia brought with them the Koran, the holy book of Islam. It teaches that there is only one god, Allah, and that Muhammad is his prophet.

TEMPLE GUARDIANS

Gilded statues of Buddhist saints ward off evil spirits at Puningsi, the Temple of Universal Peace, near Chengde. The temple was built in 1755 in the Tibetan style. It is famous for its Mahayana Hall, a tower with gilded bronze roof.

Chinese Society

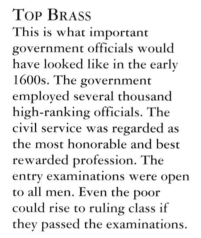

THE RIVER VALLEYS AND COASTS of China have always been among the most crowded places on earth. Confucius, with his love of social order, had taught that this vast society could be divided into four main groups. At the top were the nobles, the scholars and the landowners.

Next came the farmers, including even the poorest peasants. These people were valued because they worked for the good of the whole nation, providing the vast amounts of food necessary to feed an ever-increasing population.

In third place were skilled workers and craftsmen.

In the lowest place of all were the merchants because Confucius believed they worked for their own profit rather than for the good of the people as a whole. However, the way in which Chinese society rewarded these groups in practice did not fit the theory at all. Merchants ended up becoming the richest citizens, lending money to the upper classes. In contrast, the highly valued peasants led difficult lives, often losing their homes to floods and earthquakes or starving in years of famine.

TOP BRASS
This is what important government officials would have looked like in the early 1600s. The government employed several thousand high-ranking officials. The civil service was regarded as the most honorable and best rewarded profession. The entry examinations were open to all men. Even the poor could rise to ruling class if they passed the examinations.

THE IDEAL ORDER?
A government official tours the fields, where respectful peasants are happily at work. This painting shows an idealized view of the society proposed by Confucius. The district prospers and flourishes because everybody knows their place in society. The reality was very different—while Chinese officials led comfortable lives, most people were very poor and suffered great hardship. They toiled in the fields for little reward. Officials provided aid for the victims of famine or flood, but they never tackled the injustice of the social order. Peasant uprisings were common through much of Chinese history.

WORKING IN THE CLAYPITS

The manufacture of pottery was one of imperial China's most important industries. There were state-owned factories as well as many smaller private workshops. The industry employed some very highly skilled workers, and also thousands of unskilled laborers whose job was to dig out the precious clay. They had to work very hard for little pay. Sometimes there were serious riots to demand better working conditions.

LIFE BEHIND A DESK

Country magistrates try to remember the works of Confucius during a tough public examination. A pass would provide them with a path to wealth and social success. A failure would mean disgrace. The Chinese civil service was founded in about 900 B.C. This painting dates from the Qing dynasty (1644–1912). There were exams for all ranks of officials, and they were very difficult. The classic writings had to be remembered by heart.

DRAGON-BACKBONE MACHINE

Peasants use machinery to help work the rice fields. The life of a peasant was mostly made up of back-breaking labor. The relentless work was made slightly easier by some clever, labor-saving inventions. The square-pallet chain pump (*shown above*) was invented in about A.D. 100. It was known as the dragon-backbone machine and was used to raise water to the flooded terraces where rice was grown. Men and women worked from dawn to dusk to supply food for the population.

TOKENS OF WEALTH

Merchants may have had low social status, but they had riches beyond the dreams of peasants. They became wealthy by money-lending and by exporting luxury goods, such as silk, spices and tea. The influence of the merchant class is reflected in the first bronze Chinese coins (*c*.250 B.C.), which were shaped to look like knives, hoes and spades. Merchants commonly traded or bartered with these tools.

knife

hoe

Towns and Cities

CITIES FLOURISHED in northern China during the Shang dynasty (*c.*1600–1122 B.C.). Zhengzhou was one of the first capitals, built in about 1700 B.C. Its city wall was over four miles long, but the city spilled out far beyond this border. Chinese cities increased in size over the centuries, and by the A.D. 1500s the city of Beijing was the biggest in the world. Some great cities became centers of government, while smaller settlements served as market towns or manufacturing centers.

A typical Chinese city was surrounded by a wide moat and a high wall of packed earth. It was entered through a massive gatehouse set into the wall. The streets were filled with carts, beggars, craft workshops and street markets. Most people lived in small districts called wards that were closed off at night by locked gates. Temples and monasteries were a common sight, but royal palaces and the homes of rich families were hidden by high walls.

THE SOUND OF BELLS
Bells were set up at temples and also on towers in the cities. They were struck at daybreak to mark the opening of the gates. Big drums were struck when they were closed at night.

CHINESE SKYSCRAPERS
A pagoda (*shown far left*) soars above the skyline of a town in imperial China. Pagodas were graceful towers up to 15 stories high, with eaves projecting at each level. Buildings like these were first seen in India, where they often marked holy Buddhist sites. The Chinese perfected the design, and many people believed that pagodas spread good fortune over the surrounding land. Sometimes they were used as libraries, where scholars would study Buddhist scriptures.

MAKE A PAGODA
You will need: thick cardboard, ruler, pencil, scissors, glue and brush, masking tape, corrugated cardboard, 1¼ in x ½ in diameter dowel, embroidery bobbin, half a wooden skewer, paint (pink, terra-cotta and cream), thick and thin paintbrushes, water container.

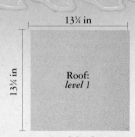

Roof: *level 1*
13¾ in / 13¾ in

Side: *level 1* (x4)
Doorway 1½ in / 3 in
11¾ in / 4½ in

Spire sides (x4)
1 in / 1¾ in / 2¾ in

(Note: The doorway is 1½ in x 3 in for all levels)

Roof: *levels 2–7*	Side (x4): *levels 2–7*
Level 2 12½ in x 12½ in	*Level 2* 10½ in x 4½ in
Level 3 11½ in x 11½ in	*Level 3* 9½ in x 4½ in
Level 4 10¼ in x 10¼ in	*Level 4* 8¼ in x 4½ in
Level 5 9 in x 9 in	*Level 5* 7 in x 4½ in
Level 6 7¾ in x 7¾ in	*Level 6* 6 in x 4½ in
Level 7 6½ in x 6½ in	*Level 7* 4¾ in x 4½ in

Cut out roof, side and spire pieces from thick cardboard.
Use the measurements shown above (pieces not to scale).

1 Start with level 1. Glue 4 side pieces together. Hold together with masking tape. Then glue pieces of cardboard behind each doorway.

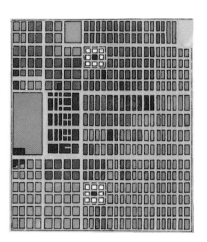

CITY PLANNING

This grid shows the layout of Chang'an (Xian), the capital city of the empire during the Tang dynasty (A.D. 618–906). The streets were grouped into small areas called wards. The design of many Chinese cities followed a similar pattern.

Lower Class ward

Middle Class ward

Upper Class ward

Government buildings

Markets

Offices

Palace

WESTERN INFLUENCE

European flags fly in the great southern port of Guangzhou, known to foreigners as Canton, in about 1810. Foreign styles of architecture appeared in some Chinese cities at this time. In the early 1800s, powerful Western countries competed to take over Chinese trade and force their policies upon the emperor.

LIVING ON THE RIM

Cities around the edge of the empire were unlike those of typical Chinese towns. The mountain city of Lhasa is the capital of Tibet. It stretches out below its towering palace, the Potala. Tibet was an independent country for much of its history, but was invaded by China in the 1700s and again in 1950.

Pagodas were built in China as early as A.D. 523. Some of the first ones were built by Chinese monks who had seen Buddhist holy temples in India. Extra stories were sometimes added on over the centuries.

2 Glue level 1 roof on top of level 1 walls. Allow to dry. Center level 2 sides on roof below. Glue down and hold with tape. Add level 2 roof.

3 Cut four 1in. wide corrugated cardboard strips for each roof. The lengths need to match the roof measures. Glue to roof and side edges.

4 Assemble levels 3 to 7. Glue together spire pieces. Wedge dowel piece into the top. Stick wooden skewer onto bobbin. Then glue bobbin onto dowel.

5 Glue spire onto top level. Use a thick brush to paint the base color. Paint details, such as terra-cotta for the roof tiles, with a thin brush.

Houses and Gardens

ALL BUILDINGS IN Chinese cities were designed to be in harmony with each other and with nature. The direction they faced, their layout and their proportions were all matters of great spiritual importance. Even the number of steps leading up to the entrance of the house was considered to be significant. House design in imperial China varied over time and between regions. In the hot and rainy south, courtyards tended to be covered to provide shade and shelter. In the drier climate of the north, courtyards were mostly open to the elements. Poor people in the countryside lived in simple, thatched huts. These were made from timber frames covered in mud plaster. They were often noisy, drafty and overcrowded. In contrast, the spacious homes of the wealthy were large, peaceful and well constructed. Many had beautiful gardens, filled with peonies, bamboo and wisteria. Some of these gardens even contained orchards, ponds and pavilions.

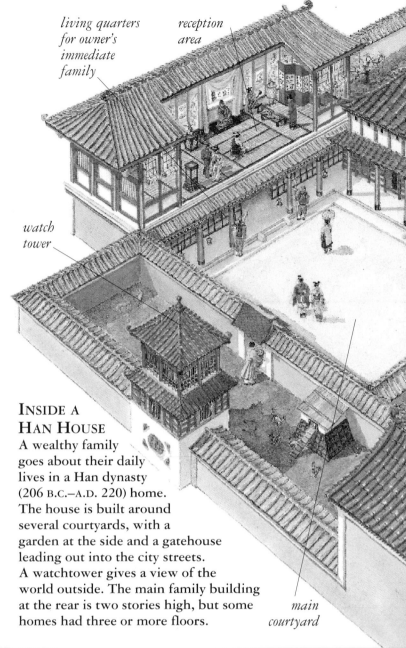

living quarters for owner's immediate family

reception area

watch tower

INSIDE A HAN HOUSE

A wealthy family goes about their daily lives in a Han dynasty (206 B.C.–A.D. 220) home. The house is built around several courtyards, with a garden at the side and a gatehouse leading out into the city streets. A watchtower gives a view of the world outside. The main family building at the rear is two stories high, but some homes had three or more floors.

main courtyard

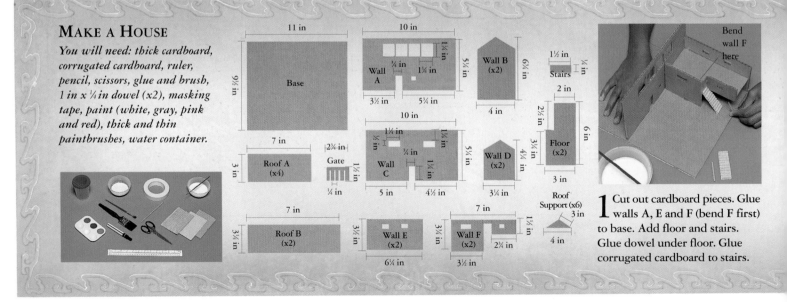

MAKE A HOUSE

You will need: thick cardboard, corrugated cardboard, ruler, pencil, scissors, glue and brush, 1 in x ¼ in dowel (x2), masking tape, paint (white, gray, pink and red), thick and thin paintbrushes, water container.

Base — 11 in, 9½ in

Roof A (x4) — 7 in, 3 in

Gate — 2¾ in, 1½ in, ¼ in

Roof B (x2) — 7 in, 3½ in

Wall A — 10 in, 5¼ in, ¾ in, 1¼ in, 1¼ in, 3½ in, 5¼ in

Wall C — 10 in, 1¼ in, ¼ in, ¾ in, 1¼ in, 1¼ in, 5¼ in, 5 in, 4½ in

Wall E (x2) — 3½ in, 6¼ in

Wall F (x2) — 7 in, 3½ in, 2¼ in, 3½ in

Wall B (x2) — 5¼ in, 6¼ in

Wall D (x2) — 3¼ in, 4¼ in

Stairs — 1½ in, ¼ in, 2 in, 4 in

Floor (x2) — 1½ in, 2½ in, 3¼ in, 6 in, 3 in

Roof Support (x6) — 3 in, 1½ in, 4 in

Bend wall F here

1 Cut out cardboard pieces. Glue walls A, E and F (bend F first) to base. Add floor and stairs. Glue dowel under floor. Glue corrugated cardboard to stairs.

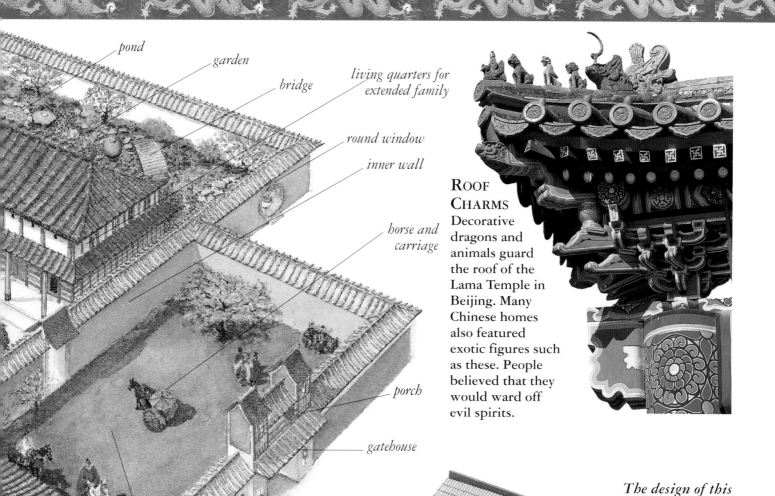

pond
garden
bridge
living quarters for
extended family
round window
inner wall
horse and
carriage
porch
gatehouse
outer wall
outer courtyard

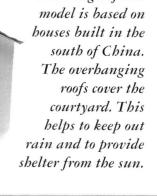

ROOF CHARMS

Decorative dragons and animals guard the roof of the Lama Temple in Beijing. Many Chinese homes also featured exotic figures such as these. People believed that they would ward off evil spirits.

The design of this model is based on houses built in the south of China. The overhanging roofs cover the courtyard. This helps to keep out rain and to provide shelter from the sun.

2 To assemble second side, repeat method described in step 1. If necessary, hold pieces together with masking tape while the glue dries.

3 Complete the walls by gluing walls B, C and D into place, as shown. Hold with tape while glue dries. Glue gate to base between wall D pieces.

4 Assemble roofs A and B. Fix supports underneath, as shown. Glue corrugated cardboard to top side of roofs (to match the roof measures).

5 Put a small piece of cardboard over the gate to make a porch. Paint house, as shown. Use a thin brush to create a tile effect on the removable roofs.

Home Comforts

A LARGE HOME in imperial China would include many living rooms for the owner and his wife, their children, the grandparents and other members of the extended family. There were several kitchens, servants' quarters, and reception rooms where guests would dine. A wealthy scholar's home would even contain its own private library.

Clay stoves provided heat in the cold northern winters. Windows were made of either stiff paper or hemp sacking instead of glass. Walls were tiled, or else decorated with beautiful silk hangings. They could be extended with carved screens. In the early days of the empire, there would be low tables, stools, urns and vases. People slept on low, heated platforms called *kang* in northern China, and the floors of homes would be covered with various mats, rugs and cushions.

Furniture making developed rapidly during the Tang dynasty (A.D. 618–906). Skilled craftsmen began producing beautiful furniture without using nails. Bamboo was widely used in the south. Instead of sitting at floor level, people began to use chairs and high tables. Elaborate furniture was made for the imperial palaces, using rosewood or woods inlaid with ivory or mother-of-pearl. Most people had furniture that was cheaper and simpler in design, but no less beautiful.

BRINGER OF LIGHT
This beautiful lamp is made of gilded bronze, and supported by the figure of a maidservant. It was found in the tomb of Liu Sheng, the Jade Prince. The lamp dates from about 100 B.C. At that time, homes were lit by oil-lamps or lanterns made of paper, silk or horn.

BEAUTY IN THE HOME
A delicate porcelain plate from the early 1700s shows a young woman standing by a table, leaning on the back of a chair. The neatly arranged books, scrolls and furniture show the importance the Chinese placed on order and harmony in the home. Chairs and tables were put against the walls. There was no clutter or mess, and possessions were always neatly put away.

FURNITURE AND FITTINGS
Richly embroidered hangings and carved tables decorate the office of this Chinese magistrate (*c.* 1600). Wealthy homes and the offices of important people often featured such luxurious decorations and furnishings.

GARDENS OF TRANQUILITY

Chinese gardens offered peace and beauty amidst the hustle and bustle of the city. Bamboo leaves rustled in the wind. Lotus flowers floated gracefully on ponds. Wisteria, with its tumbling blue flowers, wound around the summer houses. There were scented roses, peonies and chrysanthemums. Soft fruits, such as peaches and lychees, were also grown.

lychee

peach

DECORATIVE SCREEN

Standing behind the carved chair is a spectacular folding screen, made in the 1800s. Exotic paintings of landscapes, animals and birds cover its surface, while a glossy lacquer makes it smooth, hard and strong. Many wealthy homes had richly decorated wooden screens, while poorer ones had simpler, carved ones. Screens were used to keep rooms cool in summer and warm in winter.

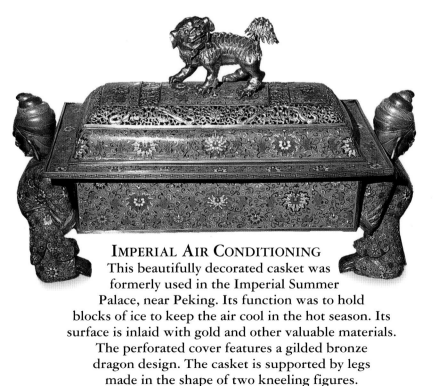

KEEPING COOL

This wine vessel was made over 3,000 years ago. It was made of bronze, which probably helped to chill the wine. Even in the earliest days of civilizations, people appreciate small luxuries and home comforts.

IMPERIAL AIR CONDITIONING

This beautifully decorated casket was formerly used in the Imperial Summer Palace, near Peking. Its function was to hold blocks of ice to keep the air cool in the hot season. Its surface is inlaid with gold and other valuable materials. The perforated cover features a gilded bronze dragon design. The casket is supported by legs made in the shape of two kneeling figures.

Family Life

KONG FUZI (CONFUCIUS) taught that just as the emperor was head of the state, the oldest man was head of the household and should be obeyed by his family. In reality, his wife ran the home and often controlled the daily lives of the other women in the household.

During the Han dynasty (206 B.C.–A.D. 220) noblewomen were kept apart from the outside world. They could only gaze at the streets from the watchtowers of their homes. It was not until the Song dynasty (A.D. 960–1279) that they gained more freedom. In poor households women worked all day, spending long, tiring hours farming, cooking, sweeping and washing.

For the children of poorer families, education meant learning to do the work their parents did. This involved carrying goods to market, or helping with the threshing or planting. The children of wealthier parents had private tutors at home. Boys hoping to become scholars or civil servants learned to read and write Chinese characters. They also studied mathematics and the works of Kong Fuzi.

LESSONS FOR THE BOYS
A group of Chinese boys do their school lessons. In imperial China, boys generally received a more academic education than girls. Girls were mainly taught music, handicrafts, painting and social skills. Some girls were taught academic subjects, but they were not allowed to take the civil service examinations.

FOOT BINDING
This foot looks elegant in its beautiful slipper, but it's a different story when the slipper is removed. Just when life was improving for Chinese women, the cruel new custom of footbinding was introduced. Dancers had bound their feet for some years in the belief that it made them look dainty. In the Song dynasty the custom spread to wealthy and noble families. Little girls of five or so had their feet bound up so tightly that they became terribly deformed.

CHINESE MARRIAGE
A wedding ceremony takes place in the late 1800s. In imperial China, weddings were arranged by the parents of the bride and groom. It was expected that the couple would respect their parents' wishes without disobedience.

TAKING IT EASY

A noblewoman living during the Qing dynasty relaxes on a garden terrace with her children, *c.* 1840. She is very fortunate to enjoy the pleasant surroundings of her home. In rich families, servants did most of the domestic work, such as cooking, cleaning and washing. Wealthy Chinese families kept many servants, who usually lived in quarters inside their employer's home. Servants accounted for a large number of the workforce in imperial China. During the Ming dynasty (1368–1644), some 9,000 maidservants were employed at the imperial palace in Beijing alone!

RESPECT AND HONOR

Children in the 1100s bow respectfully to their parents. Confucius taught that people should value and honor their families, including their ancestors. He believed that this helped to create a more orderly and virtuous society.

THE EMPEROR AND HIS MANY WIVES

Sui dynasty Emperor Yangdi (A.D. 581–618) rides with an entourage of women. Like many emperors, Yangdi was often surrounded by women. An emperor married one woman, who would then become his empress, but he would still enjoy the company of concubines (secondary wives).

Farming and Crops

EIGHT THOUSAND YEARS AGO the majority of Chinese people lived by farming. The best soil lay beside the great rivers in central and eastern China, where floods left behind rich, fertile mud. As today, wheat and millet were grown in the north. This region was mostly farmed by peasants with small plots of land. Rice was cultivated in the warm, wet south, where wealthy city-dwellers owned large estates. Pears and oranges were grown in orchards.

Tea, later to become one of China's most famous exports, was first cultivated about 1,700 years ago. Hemp was also grown for its fibers. During the 500s B.C., cotton was introduced. Farmers raised pigs, ducks, chickens and geese, while oxen and water buffalo were used as labor animals on the farm.

Most peasants used basic tools, such as stone hoes and wooden rakes. Ploughs with iron blades were used from about 600 B.C. Other inventions to help farmers were developed in the next few hundred years, including the wheelbarrow, a pedal hammer for husking grain and a rotary winnowing fan.

PIGS ARE FARM FAVORITES

This pottery model of pigs in their sty dates back about 2,000 years. Pigs were popular farm animals, as they are easy to feed and most parts of a pig can be eaten. They were kept in the city as well as in rural country areas.

FEEDING THE MANY

Rice has been grown in the wetter regions of China since ancient times. Wheat and millet are grown in the drier regions. Sprouts of the Indian mung bean add important vitamins to many dishes.

mung beans

millet

rice

wheat

CHINESE TEAS

Delicate tea leaves are picked from the bushes and gathered in large baskets on this estate in the 1800s. The Chinese cultivated tea in ancient times, but it became much more popular during the Tang dynasty (A.D. 618–906). The leaves were picked, laid out in the sun, rolled by hand and then dried over charcoal fires.

WORKING THE LAND

A farmer uses a pair of strong oxen to help him plow his land. This wall painting found in Jiayuguan dates back to about 100 B.C. Oxen saved farmers a lot of time and effort. The Chinese first used oxen in farming in about 1122 B.C.

KEEPING WARM

This model of a Chinese farmer's lambing shed dates from about 100 B.C., during the Han dynasty. Sheepskins were worn for warmth, but wool never became an important textile for clothes or blankets in China.

HARVESTING RICE—CHINA'S STAPLE FOOD

Chinese peasants pull up rice plants for threshing and winnowing in the 1600s. Farming methods were passed on by word of mouth and in handbooks from the earliest times. They advised farmers on everything from fertilizing the soil to controlling pests.

A TIMELESS SCENE

Peasants bend over to plant rows of rice seedlings in the flooded rice paddies of Yunnan province, in southwest China. This modern photograph is a typical scene of agricultural life in China's warm and wet southwest region. Little has changed in hundreds of years of farming.

Fine Food

CHINESE COOKS TODAY are among the best in the world, with skills gained over thousands of years. Rice was the basis of most meals in ancient China, especially in the south where it was grown. Northerners used wheat flour to make noodles and buns. Food varied greatly between the regions. The north was famous for pancakes, dumplings, lamb and duck dishes. In the west, Sichuan was renowned for its hot chile peppers. Mushrooms and bamboo shoots were popular along the lower Chang Jiang (Yangzi River).

For many people, meat dishes were a rare treat. They included chicken, pork and many kinds of fish, and were often spiced with garlic and ginger. Dishes featured meat that people from other parts of the world might find exotic, such as turtle, dog, monkey and bear. Food was stewed, steamed or fried. The use of chopsticks and bowls dates back to the Shang dynasty (*c.* 1600–1122 B.C.).

THE KITCHEN GOD
In every kitchen hung a paper picture of the kitchen god and his wife. Each year, on the 24th day of the 12th month, candies were presented as offerings. Then the picture was taken down and burned. A new one was put in its place on New Year's Day.

A TANG BANQUET
These elegant ladies of the Tang court are sitting down to a feast. They are accompanied by music and singing, but there are no men present—women and men usually ate separately. This painting dates from the 900s, when raised tables came into fashion in China. Guests at banquets would wear their finest clothes. The most honored guest would sit to the east of the host, who sat facing the south. The greatest honor of all was to be invited to dine with the emperor.

MAKE RED BEAN SOUP
You will need: measuring cups, scales, measuring spoons, 7¼ oz adzuki beans, 3 tsp peanuts, 4 tsp short-grain rice, cold water, tangerine, saucepan and lid, wooden spoon, 5½ oz sugar, blender, sieve, bowls.

1 Use the scale to weigh the adzuki beans. Add the peanuts and the short-grain rice. Measure out 4¼ cups of cold water.

2 Wash and drain the beans and rice. Put them in a bowl. Add the cold water. Let soak. Do not drain off the water.

3 Wash and dry the tangerine. Then carefully take off the peel in a continuous strip. Let the tangerine peel stay out over night, until it is hard and dry.

THAT SPECIAL TASTE

Garlic has been used to flavor Chinese dishes and sauces for thousands of years. It may be chopped, crushed, pickled or served whole. Ginger is another crucial Chinese taste. Fresh chile peppers are used to make fiery dishes, while sesame provides flavoring in the form of paste, oil and seeds.

ginger

sesame

SHANG BRONZEWARE FIT FOR A FEAST

This three-legged bronze cooking pot dates from the Shang dynasty (*c.*1600 B.C.–1122 B.C.). Its green appearance is caused by the reaction of the metal to air (oxidation) over the 3,500 years since it was made. During Shang rule, metalworkers made many vessels out of bronze, including cooking pots and wine jars. They were used in all sorts of ceremonies, including at feasts to honor their dead ancestors.

BUTCHERS AT WORK

The stone carving *(shown right)* shows farmers butchering cattle in about A.D. 50. In early China, cooks would cut up meat with square-shaped cleavers. It was then flavored with wines and spices, and simmered in big pots over open fires until tender.

Most peasant farmers lived on a simple diet. Red bean soup with rice was a typical daily meal. Herbs and spices were often added to make the food taste more interesting.

4 Put the soaked beans and rice (plus the soaking liquid) into a large saucepan. Add the dried tangerine peel and another 2¼ cups of cold water.

5 Bring the mixture to a boil. Reduce the heat, cover the saucepan and simmer for 2 hours. Stir occasionally. If the liquid boils off, add more water.

6 Weigh the sugar. When the beans are just covered by water, add the sugar. Simmer until the sugar has completely dissolved.

7 Remove and discard the tangerine peel. Let soup cool, uncovered. Ask an adult to blend the mixture. Strain any lumps with a sieve. Pour into bowls.

Markets and Trade

THE EARLIEST CHINESE TRADERS used to barter (exchange) goods, but by 1600 B.C. people were finding it easier to use tokens such as shells for buying and selling. The first metal coins date from about 750 B.C. and were shaped like knives and spades. It was Qin Shi Huangdi, the first emperor, who introduced round metal coins. These had holes in the middle so that they could be threaded on to a cord for safe-keeping. The world's first paper money appeared in China in about A.D. 900.

There were busy markets in every Chinese town, selling fruit, vegetables, rice, flour, eggs and poultry as well as cloth, medicine, pots and pans. In the Tang dynasty capital Chang'an (Xian), trading was limited to two large areas—the West Market and the East Market. This was so government officials could control prices and trading standards.

CHINESE TRADING
Goods from China changed hands many times on the Silk Road to Europe. Trade moved in both directions. Porcelain, tea and silk were carried westward. Silver, gold and precious stones were transported back into China from central and southern Asia.

raw silk   *Chinese tea*

CASH CROPS
The fascination of tea with Europeans inspired this fantastic image of Chinese tea productions. For years China had traded with India and Arabia. In the 1500s it began a continuous trading relationship with Europe. By the early 1800s, China supplied 90 percent of all the world's tea.

MAKE A PELLET DRUM

You will need: large roll of masking tape, pencil, thin cream card stock, thick cardboard, scissors, glue and brush, 1 in. x 11¾ in. thin gray card stock, thread, ruler, needle, bamboo stick, paint (red, green and black), water container, paintbrush, 2 colored beads.

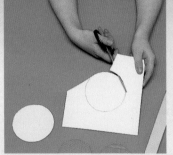

1 Use the outside of a large tape roll to draw 2 circles on thin cream card stock. Use the inside to draw 2 smaller circles on thick cardboard. Cut out as shown.

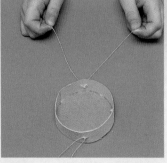

2 Glue gray strip around one of smaller circles. Make 2 small holes each side of strip. Cut two 8 in. threads. Pass one through each pair of holes.

3 Knot threads to tie them to strip. Use scissors to make a hole in the side for the bamboo stick. Push stick through. Tape stick into position.

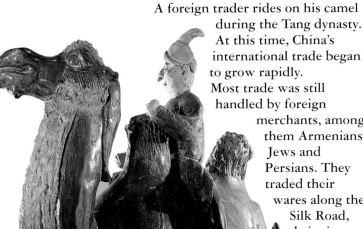

FROM DISTANT LANDS

A foreign trader rides on his camel during the Tang dynasty. At this time, China's international trade began to grow rapidly. Most trade was still handled by foreign merchants, among them Armenians, Jews and Persians. They traded their wares along the Silk Road, bringing goods to the court at the Tang dynasty capital, Chang'an.

THE SILK ROAD

The trading route known as the Silk Road developed during the Han dynasty. The road ran for 6,800 mi. from Chang'an (modern Xian), through Yumen and Kasghar, to Persia and the shores of the Mediterranean Sea. Merchants carried tea, silk and other goods from one trading post to the next.

BUYERS AND SELLERS

This picture shows a typical Chinese market in about 1100. It appears on a Song dynasty scroll, and is thought to show the market in the capital, Kaifeng, at the time of the New Year festival.

Twist the drum handle to make the little balls rattle. In the hubbub of a street market, a merchant could shake a pellet drum to gain the attention of passers-by. He would literally drum up trade!

4 Tape the stick handle down securely at the top of the drum. Take the second small circle and glue it firmly into place. This seals the drum.

5 Draw matching designs of your choice on the 2 thin cream card stock circles. Cut out a decorative edge. Paint in the designs and let them dry.

6 Paint the bamboo stick handle red and let dry. When the stick is dry, glue the 2 decorated circles into position on top of the 2 smaller circles.

7 Thread on the 2 beads. Make sure the thread is long enough to allow the beads to hit the center of the drum. Tie as shown. Cut off any excess.

Medicine and Science

Fʀᴏᴍ ᴛʜᴇ ᴇᴍᴘɪʀᴇ's earliest days, Chinese scholars published studies on medicine, astronomy and mathematics. The Chinese system of medicine had a similar aim to that of Daoist teachings, in that it attempted to make the body function harmoniously. The effects of all kinds of herbs, plants and animal parts were studied and then used to produce medicines. Acupuncture, which involves piercing the body with fine needles, was practiced from about 2700 B.C. It was believed to release blocked channels of energy and so relieve pain.

The Chinese were also excellent mathematicians, and from 300 B.C. they used a decimal system of counting based on tens. They may have invented the abacus, an early form of a calculator, as well. In about 3000 B.C., Chinese astronomers produced a detailed chart of the heavens carved in stone. Later, they were the first to make observations of sunspots and exploding stars.

NEW ILLS, OLD REMEDIES
A pharmacist weighs out a traditional medicine. Hundreds of medicines used in China today go back to ancient times. Some are herbal remedies later proved to work by scientists. Doctors are still researching their uses. Other traditional medicines are of less certain value, but are still popular purchases at street stalls.

PRICKING POINTS
Acupuncturists used charts (*shown above*) to show exactly where to position their needles. The vital qi (energy) was thought to flow through the body along 12 lines called meridians. The health of the patient was judged by taking their pulse. Chinese acupuncture is practiced all over the world today.

MAKE AN ABACUS
You will need: thick and thin cardboard, ruler, pencil, scissors, wood glue and brush, masking tape, self-drying clay, cutting board, modeling tool, 11¼ in. x ¼ in. dowel (x11), paintbrush, water container, brown paint.

Side A (x2) — 12½ in — 1¼ in

Edge A (x2) — 12½ in / 11¾ in — ¼ in

Side B (x2) — 6¼ in — 6¼ in

Edge B (x2) — 6¼ in / 6 in — ⅛ in

Base — 12½ in — 6¼ in

Divider / Divider edge — 11½ in — 1¼ in / ¼ in

Using the above measurements, cut out pieces from thick brown cardboard and thin gray cardboard. (pieces not shown to scale).

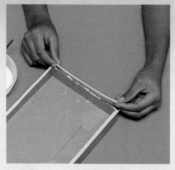

1 Glue sides A and B to the base. Hold the edges with masking tape until dry. Then glue edges A and B to the tops of the sides, as shown.

2 Roll the clay into a ¾ in. diameter sausage. Cut into 77 small, flat beads. Make a hole through the center of each bead with a dowel.

A STREET DOCTOR PEDDLES HIS CURES
This European view of Chinese medicine dates from 1843. It shows snakes and all sorts of unusual potions being sold on the streets. The doctor is telling the crowd of miraculous cures.

NATURAL HEALTH
Roots, seeds, leaves and flowers have been used in Chinese medicine for over 2,000 years. Today, nine out of ten Chinese medicines are herbal remedies. The Chinese yam is used to treat exhaustion. Ginseng root is used to help treat dizzy spells, while mulberry wood is said to lower blood pressure.

Chinese yam

ginseng root

BURNING CURES
A country doctor treats a patient with traditional techniques during the Song dynasty. Chinese doctors relieved pain by heating parts of the body with the burning leaves of a plant called moxa (mugwort). The process is called moxibustion.

The abacus is an ancient counting frame that acts as a simple but very effective calculator. Using an abacus, Chinese mathematicians and merchants could carry out very difficult calculations quickly and easily.

3 Make 11 evenly spaced holes in the divider. Edge one side with thin cardboard. Then thread a dowel through each hole. Paint all of the abacus parts. Let dry.

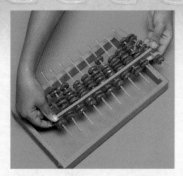

4 Thread 7 beads onto each dowel rod—2 on the upper side of the divider, 5 on the lower. Carefully fit the beads and rods into the main frame.

5 Each upper bead on the abacus equals 5 lower beads in the same column. Each lower bead is worth 10 of the lower beads in the column to its right.

6 Here is a simple sum. To calculate 5+3, first move down one upper bead (worth 5). Then move 3 lower beads in the same column up (each worth 1).

Feats of Engineering

THE ENGINEERING WONDER of ancient China was the Great Wall. It was known as *Wan Li Chang Cheng*, or the Wall of Ten Thousand *Li* (a unit of length). The Great Wall's main length was an incredible 2,485 miles. Work began on the wall in the 400s B.C. and lasted until the A.D. 1500s. Its purpose was to protect China's borders from the fierce tribes who lived to the north. Despite this intention, Mongol invaders managed to penetrate its defenses time after time. However, the Great Wall did serve as a useful communications route. It also extended the Chinese empire's control over a very long distance.

The Grand Canal is another engineering project that amazes us today. It was started in about 400s B.C., but was mostly built during the Sui dynasty (A.D. 581–618). Its aim was to link the north of China with the rice-growing regions in the south, via the Chang Jiang (Yangzi River). It is still in use and runs northward from Hangzhou to Beijing, a distance of 1,115 miles. Other great engineering feats were made by Chinese mining engineers, who were already digging deep mine shafts with drainage and ventilation systems in about 160 B.C.

LIFE IN THE SALT MINES
Workers busily excavate and purify salt from an underground mine. Inside a tower (*shown bottom left*) you can see workers using a pulley to raise baskets of mined salt. The picture comes from a relief (raised carving) found inside a Han dynasty tomb in the province of Sichuan.

MINING ENGINEERING
A Qing dynasty official tours an open-cast coal mine in the 1800s. China has rich natural resources, and may have been the first country in the world to mine coal to burn as fuel. Coal was probably discovered in about 200 B.C. in what is now Jiangxi province. Other mines extracted metals and valuable minerals needed for the great empire. In the Han dynasty engineers invented methods of drilling boreholes to extract brine (salty water) from the ground. They also used derricks (rigid frameworks) to support iron drills—over 1,800 years before engineers in other parts of the world.

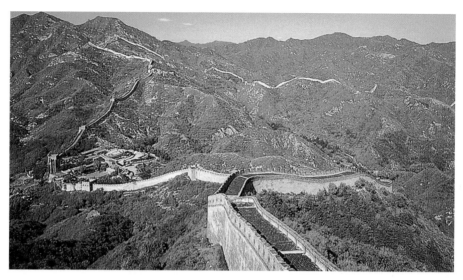

HARD LABOR
Peasants use their spades to dig roads instead of fields. Imperial China produced its great buildings and engineering works without the machines we rely on today. For big projects, workforces could number in the hundreds of thousands. Dangerous working conditions and a harsh climate killed many laborers.

BUILDING THE WALL
The Great Wall snakes over mountain ridges at Badaling, to the northwest of Beijing. The Great Wall and Grand Canal were built by millions of workers. All men aged between 23 and 56 were called to work on them for one month each year. Only noblemen and civil servants were exempt.

A GRAND OPENING
This painting from the 1700s imagines the Sui emperor Yangdi opening the first stage of the Grand Canal. Most of the work on this massive engineering project was carried out from A.D. 605–609. A road was also built along the route. The transport network built up during the Sui dynasty (561–618 A.D.) enabled food and other supplies to be moved easily from one part of the empire to another.

THE CITY OF SIX THOUSAND BRIDGES
The reports about China allegedly made by Marco Polo in the 1200s described 6,000 bridges in the city of Suzhou. The Baodai Bridge (*shown above*) is one of them. It has 53 arches and was built between A.D. 618 and A.D. 906 to run across the Grand Canal.

Famous Inventions

WHEN YOU WALK DOWN a commercial street in any modern city, it is very difficult to avoid seeing some object that was invented in China long ago. Printed words on paper, silk scarves, umbrellas and locks and keys are all Chinese innovations. Over the centuries, Chinese ingenuity and technical skill have changed the world in which we live.

A seismoscope is a very useful instrument in an earthquake-prone country such as China. It was invented in A.D. 132 by a Chinese scientist named Zhang Heng. It could record the direction of even a distant earth tremor.

Another key invention was the magnetic compass. In about A.D. 1–100 the Chinese discovered that lodestone (a type of iron ore) could be made to point north. They realized that they could magnetize needles to do the same. By about A.D. 1000, they figured out the difference between true north and magnetic north, and began using compasses to keep ships on course.

Gunpowder is a Chinese invention from about A.D. 850. At first it was used to blast rocks apart and to make fireworks. Later, it also began to be used in warfare.

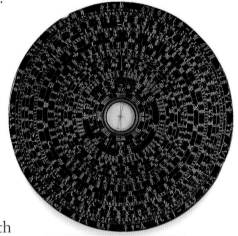

THE SAILOR'S FRIEND
The magnetic compass was invented in China in about A.D. 1–100. At first it was used as a planning aid to ensure that new houses faced in a direction that was in harmony with nature. Later it was used to plot courses on long sea voyages.

SHADE AND SHELTER
A Qing dynasty woman uses an umbrella as a sunshade to protect her skin. The Chinese invented umbrellas about 1,600 years ago, and they soon spread throughout the rest of Asia. Umbrellas became fashionable with both women and men and were regarded as a symbol of high rank.

MAKE A WHEELBARROW

You will need: thick cardboard, ruler, pencil, scissors, compass, ¼ in. diameter balsa strips, glue and brush, paintbrush, paint (black and brown), water container, 1½ in. x ¼ in. dowel, ¾ in. diameter rubber washers (x4).

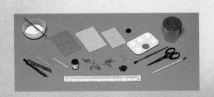

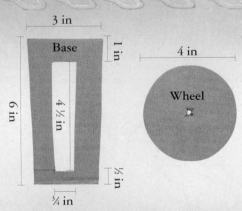

Using the measurements above, draw the pieces onto thick cardboard. Draw the wheel with the compass. Cut out pieces with scissors.

SU SONG'S MASTERPIECE

This fantastic machine is a clock tower that can tell the time, chime the hours and follow the movement of the planets around the sun. It was designed by an official named Su Song, in the city of Kaifeng in A.D. 1092. The machine uses a mechanism called an escapement, which controls and regulates the timing of the clock. The escapement mechanism was invented in the A.D. 700s by a Chinese inventor named Yi Xing.

EARTHQUAKE WARNING

The decorative object shown above is the scientist Zhang Heng's seismoscope. When there was an earthquake, a ball was released from one of the dragons and fell into a frog's mouth. This showed the direction of the vibrations. According to records, in A.D. 138 the instrument detected an earth tremor some 310 miles away.

ONE-WHEELED TRANSPORT

In about A.D. 100, the Chinese invented the wheelbarrow. They then designed a model with a large central wheel that could bear great weights. This became a form of transport, pushed along by muscle power.

The single wheelbarrow was used by farmers and gardeners. Traders wheeled their goods to market, then used the barrow as a stall. They would sell a variety of goods, such as seeds, grain, plants and dried herbs.

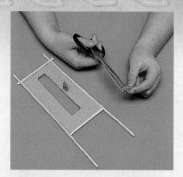

2 Turn the barrow over. Cut two ¾ in. x ½ in. pieces of thick cardboard. Make a small hole in the middle of each, for the wheel axle. Glue pieces to base.

3 Use a compass and a pencil to draw one circle around center of wheel and one close to the rim. Mark on spokes. Paint spaces between spokes black.

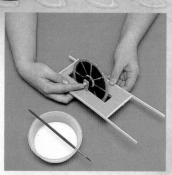

4 Paint the barrow and leave to dry. Cut two 2¾ in. balsa strips with tapered ends to make legs. Paint brown. When dry, glue to bottom of barrow.

5 Feed dowel axle between axle supports, via 2 washers, wheel, and 2 more washers. Dab glue on ends of axle, to allow wheel to spin without falling off.

Stone Relics

CHINESE CIVILIZATION BEGAN over 5,000 years ago in the Neolithic period (New Stone Age). Stone was one of the first materials to be worked. It was used to make practical objects, such as hand mills for grinding grain or tools for the farm, as well as for ornaments.

The Chinese valued one type of stone above all others—jade. Many figures and statues were made of the stone. People thought it had magical properties and could preserve the dead. The Han dynasty prince Liu Sheng and his wife, Dou Wan, were buried in suits made of over 2,000 thin jade plates sewn together with gold wire.

On a very different scale, the spread of Buddhism led to the popularity of gigantic stone sculptures. The Great Buddha above the town of Leshan, Sichuan, was carved into the rock in the A.D. 700s. It is 230 feet high and took 90 years to carve from the rockface. Inside, a system of drains helps to prevent the stone from weathering.

BUFFALO IN JADE
Water buffalo were highly prized animals in imperial China. This beautiful carving measures about 17 inches in length. It was carved from a single large piece of jade during the 1300s. The precious stone was mined in the northwest of the country, in the region that is now known as Xinjiang.

STONY ELEPHANT
The symbolically carved elephant (*shown above*) is one of many statues of animals that line the 4½ miles of the Spirit Way. This is a ceremonial avenue that leads to the Ming tombs at Shisanling, to the north of Beijing. The elephant statue was carved during the 1400s.

MARBLE BOAT
This boat will never sail! It was commissioned by Empress Dowager Cixi, and completed in the last days of her empire in 1908. She used funds meant for the navy to build this marble boat at her Summer Palace in Yiheyuan.

THE AFTERLIFE

This stone statue is one of many that guard the tombs at Shisanling, north of Beijing. Yong Li and 12 other Ming emperors were buried here from the 1400s onwards. The statues were made in the form of both humans and animals. They were probably placed there to protect each emperor in his next life.

CARVED FROM ROCK

A great Buddha dominates the spectacular stone carvings of the Yungang cave temples. It is located in what is now Shanxi province, northern China. The huge figure is some 49 feet in height. The elaborate stone carvings at the caves were completed at some point between A.D. 460 and the early A.D. 500s. In total, they take up half a mile of the rockface.

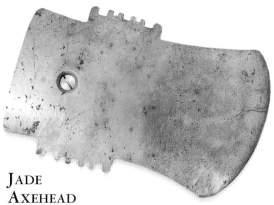

JADE AXEHEAD

Simple decorative notches are carved onto this Shang dynasty jade axehead. Jade is a tough and difficult stone to cut. Early craftsmen did not have sharp enough tools to cut more detailed or elaborate patterns.

JADE DISCS

Bi are large discs made of jade. The one shown here measures about 10½ inches in diameter. *Bi* were usually hung from cords of silk and were meant to represent heaven. These patterned discs were worn by priests at ceremonies from about 2500 B.C. until Han times.

Metalworking

BEWARE OF THE LION
This gilded *fo* (Buddhist) lion guards the halls and chambers of Beijing's imperial palace, the Forbidden City. It is one of a fearsome collection of bronze guardian figures, including statues of dragons and turtles.

THE CHINESE MASTERED THE secrets of making alloys (mixtures of two or more metals) during the Shang dynasty (*c.* 1600 B.C.–1122 B.C.). They made bronze by melting copper and tin to separate each metal from its ore, a process called smelting. Nine parts of copper were then mixed with one part of tin and heated in a charcoal furnace. When the metals melted they were poured into clay molds. Bronze was used to make objects such as ceremonial pots, statues, bells, mirrors, tools and weapons.

By about 600 B.C. the Chinese were smelting iron ore. They became the first people to make cast iron by adding carbon to the molten metal.

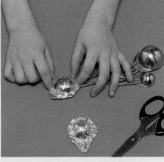

SILVER SCISSORS
This pair of scissors is made of silver. They are proof of the foreign influences that entered China in the A.D. 700s, during the boom years of the Tang dynasty. The metal is beaten, rather than cast in the Chinese way. It is decorated in the Persian style of the Silk Road with engraving and punching.

Cast iron is a tougher metal than bronze and it was soon being used to make weapons, tools and plough blades. By A.D. 1000 the Chinese were mining and working a vast amount of iron. Coke (a type of coal) had replaced the charcoal used in furnaces, which were fired up by water-driven bellows. Chinese metal workers also produced delicate gold and silver ornaments set with precious stones.

MAKE A NECKLACE

You will need: tape measure, thick wire, thin wire, masking tape, scissors, tinfoil, measuring spoon, glue and brush, fuse wire.

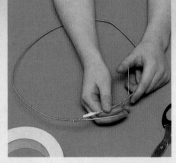

1 Measure around your neck using a tape measure. Ask an adult to cut a piece of thick wire to 1½ times this length. Shape it into a rough circle.

2 Cut two 1½ in. pieces of thin wire. Coil loosely around sides of thick wire. Tape ends to thick wire. Slide thick wire through coils to adjust fit.

3 Cut out an oval-shaped piece of tinfoil. Shape it into a pendant half, using a measuring spoon or teaspoon. Make 9 more halves.

MINERAL WEALTH

The Chinese probably learned to smelt ore in furnaces from their experience with high-temperature pottery kilns. The land was rich in copper, tin and iron, and the Chinese were very skilled miners. Large amounts of precious metals, such as gold and silver, had to be imported.

gold nugget *silver ore*

DECORATIVE PROTECTION

These nail protectors are made of gold, with inlaid feathers. They were worn by the Empress Dowager Cixi in the 1800s on both her little fingers to prevent her 6 inch-long nails from breaking.

PEACE BE WITH YOU

The Hall of Supreme Harmony in Beijing's Forbidden City is guarded by this bronze statue of a turtle. Despite its rather fearsome appearance, the turtle was actually a symbol of peace.

GOLDEN FIREBIRDS

Chinese craftsmen fashioned these beautiful phoenix birds from thin sheets of delicate gold. The mythical Arabian phoenix was said to set fire to its nest and die, only to rise again from the ashes. During the Tang dynasty the phoenix became a symbol of the Chinese empress Wu Zetian, who came to power in A.D. 660. It later came to be a more general symbol for all empresses.

4 Glue the 2 pendant halves together, leaving one end open. Drop some rolled-up balls of foil into the opening. Seal the opening with glue.

5 Make 4 more pendants in the same way. Thread each pendant onto the neckband with pieces of thin fuse wire. Leave a gap between each one.

People of all classes wore decorative jewelry in imperial China. The design of this necklace is based on the metal bell bracelets worn by Chinese children.

39

Porcelain and Lacquer

ALTHOUGH POTTERY FIRST developed in Japan and parts of western Asia, Chinese potters were hard at work over 6,000 years ago. In 3200 B.C., clay was being fired (baked) in kilns at about 1,600°F.

By 1400 B.C., potters were making beautiful, white stoneware, baked at much higher temperatures. Shiny glazes were developed to coat the fired clay. Later, the Chinese invented porcelain, the finest, most delicate pottery of all. It was to become one of China's most important exports to other parts of Asia and Europe. In the English language, the word china is used for all fine-quality pottery.

The Chinese were the first to use lacquer. This plastic-like material is a substance from the sap of a tree that grows in China. The sap makes a smooth, hard varnish. Beginning in about 1300 B.C., lacquer was used to coat wooden surfaces, such as house timbers, bowls or furniture. It could also be applied to leather and metal. Natural lacquer is gray, but in China pigment was added to make it black or bright red. It was applied in many layers until thick enough to be carved or inlaid with mother-of-pearl.

ENAMEL WARE
Ming dynasty craft workers made this ornate flask. It is covered with a glossy material called enamel, set inside thin metal wire. This technique, called cloisonné, was introduced from Persia.

CHINA'S HISTORY TOLD ON THE BIG SCREEN
This beautifully detailed, glossy lacquer screen shows a group of Portuguese merchants on a visit to China. It was made in the 1600s. Chinese crafts first became popular in Europe at this time, as European traders began doing business in southern China's ports.

FLORAL BOTTLE
This attractive Ming dynasty bottle is decorated with a coating of bright red lacquer. The lacquer is colored with a mineral called cinnabar. It would have taken many long hours to apply and dry the many layers of lacquer. The bottle is carved with a design of peonies, which were very popular flowers in China.

FISH ON A PLATE

Pictures of fish decorate the border of this precious porcelain plate. It was made during the reign of the Qing emperor Yongzheng (1722–1736), a period famous for its elegant designs. It is colored with enamel. Porcelain is made from a fine white clay called kaolin (china clay) and a mineral called feldspar. They are fired (baked) at a very high temperature.

A JUG OF WINE

An unknown Chinese potter made this beautiful wine jug about 1,000 years ago. It has been fired to such a high temperature that it has become glassy stoneware. It is coated with a gray-green glaze called celadon.

LIFE-LIKE FIGURES

A Ming dynasty entertainer smiles at his audience. All sorts of pottery figures have been found in Ming dynasty tombs. Potters made lively figures of merchants, musicians, court ladies and animals. Some are comic, while others are beautiful.

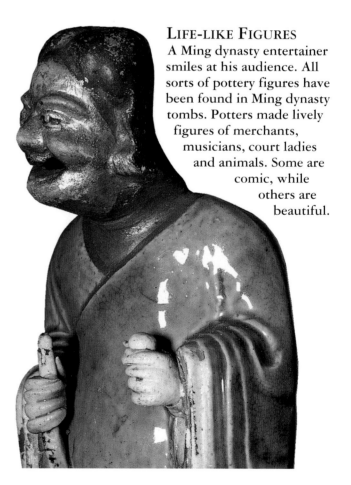

DEEP BLUE, PURE WHITE

These blue-and-white vases are typical of the late Ming dynasty (1368–1644). In the 1600s large numbers were exported to Europe. Many were produced at the imperial potteries at Jingdezhen, in northern Jiangxi province. These workshops were set up in 1369, as the region was an abundant source of the very best clay. Some of the finest pottery ever made was produced there in the 1400s and 1500s.

The Secret of Silk

For years, the Chinese tried to prevent outsiders from finding out how they made their most popular export—*si*, or silk. The shimmering colors and smooth textures of Chinese silk made it the wonder of the ancient world. Other countries such as India discovered the secret of silk making, but China remained the producer of the world's best silk.

Silk production probably dates back to the late Stone Age period (8000 B.C.–2500 B.C.) in China. Legend says that the process was invented by the Empress Lei Zu in about 2640 B.C. Silkworms (the caterpillars of a type of moth) are kept on trays and feed on the leaves of white mulberry trees. The silkworms spin a cocoon (casing) of fine but very strong filaments. The cocoons are plunged into boiling water to separate the filaments, which are then carefully wound onto reels.

A filament of silk can be up to 4,000 feet long. Several filaments are spun together to make thread, which is then woven into cloth on a loom. The Chinese used silk to make all kinds of beautiful products. They learned to weave flimsy gauzes and rich brocades and then weave elaborate, colored patterns into the cloth in a style known as *ke si*, or cut silk.

Preparing the Thread

A young woman winds silk thread onto bobbins in the late 1700s. Up to 30 filaments of silk could be twisted together to make silk thread for weaving. The Chinese made ingenious equipment for spinning silk into thread. They also built looms for weaving thread into large rolls of fabric. By the 1600s, the city of Nanjing alone had an estimated 50,000 looms.

Loading Bales!

Workers at a Chinese silk factory of the 1840s carry large bales of woven silk down to the jetty. From there the woven cloth would be shipped to the city. It might be used to make a costume for a lady of the court, or else exported abroad. The Chinese silk industry reached its peak of prosperity in the mid-1800s.

WINDING SILK

Silk is being prepared at this workshop in the 1600s. The workers are taking filaments (threads) from the cocoons and winding them onto a reel. Traditionally, the chief areas of silk production in imperial China were in the east coast provinces of Zhejiang and Jiangsu. Silk was also produced in large quantities in Sichuan, in the west.

THE DRAGON ON THE EMPEROR'S BACK

A scaly red dragon writhes across a sea of yellow silk. The dragon was embroidered onto a robe for an emperor of the Qing dynasty. The exquisite clothes made for the Chinese imperial court at this time are considered to be great works of art.

MAKING SILK

Raising silkworms is called sericulture. It can be a complicated business. The caterpillars have to be kept at a controlled temperature for a month before they begin spinning their silk cocoons.

adult silkmoth and cocoons

silkmoth larva

MAGIC MULBERRIES

These Han dynasty workers are collecting mulberry leaves in big baskets, over 2,000 years ago. These would have been used to feed the silkworms. Silkworms are actually the larva (caterpillars) of a type of moth. Like most caterpillars, silkworms are fussy feeders and will only eat certain kinds of plant before they spin cocoons.

Dress and Ornament

CHINESE PEASANTS dressed in simple clothes made from basic materials. They mostly wore cotton tunics over loose trousers, with sandals made of rushes or straw. In the south, broad-brimmed, cone-shaped hats helped to protect the wearer from the hot sun and heavy rain. In the north, fur hats, sheepskins and quilted jackets were worn to keep out the cold. Rich people dressed elaborately. The style and even the color of dress was laid down by law and showed social status. Merchants, for example, were not allowed to wear silk. Only emperors could wear yellow, or official robes of silk patterned with dragons.

Court dress varied greatly over the ages. Foreign invasions brought new fashions and dress codes. Under the Manchus, who ruled as the Qing dynasty from A.D. 1644, men had to wear a long pigtail. Rich people grew their little fingernails so long that special nail guards were worn to prevent them from breaking off.

CLOTHES FIT FOR AN EMPEROR
This magnificent imperial robe was made from interwoven, heavy silks in the 1800s. The narrow sleeves, with their horse hoof cuffs, are typical of the Qing dynasty.

MONKEY PENDANT
Wealthy people often wore very expensive, well-crafted jewelry. This beautiful piece from the A.D. 700s is a pendant necklace. It could have been worn by both men and women. The pendant is made from white jade set in a beaded frame of gilded bronze.

FASTEN YOUR BELT
Belt hooks and buckles became an essential part of noblemen's clothing from about the 300s B.C. They were highly decorated, and made of bronze.

MAKE A FAN

You will need: masking tape, red tissue paper, thick cardboard base, ruler, pencil, compass, paint (pink, light blue, cream, light green), thin paintbrush, water container, scissors, 6¼ in. x ½ in. balsa strips (x15), wooden skewers, glue and brush, thin cardboard.

1 Tape tissue paper onto base. Make a compass hole ½ in. from the edge. From this mark, draw a 6 in. radius semicircle and a 2¾ in. radius semicircle.

2 Place one end of the ruler at compass hole. Mark the point with a pencil. Draw evenly spaced lines ½ in. apart between the semi-circles.

3 Draw your design onto the tissue paper. Paint in the details. Let dry. Remove paper from base. Cut out fan along edges of the semicircles.

OFFICIAL DRESS

A well-dressed civil servant cools down in the summer heat. Chinese government officials wore elegant clothes that showed their social rank. This picture was painted by a European artist in about 1800. The official is wearing his summer outfit, which consists of a long narrow-sleeved tunic, slippers and a brimmed hat. He also carries a fan to provide a cool breeze.

LADIES OF THE COURT

These Tang ladies are dressed in the high fashion of the A.D. 700s. Silk was the material worn by the nobles of the day, and court costume included long robes and skirts, various tunics and sashes. The clothes were often beautifully decorated with colorful patterns and elaborate designs.

ADDED STYLE

Over the ages, all kinds of accessories became part of Chinese costume. These included elaborate hats and headdresses for men and women, sunshades, fans, belts and buckles. Tiny leather shoes lined with silk were worn by noblewomen.

ladies' shoes

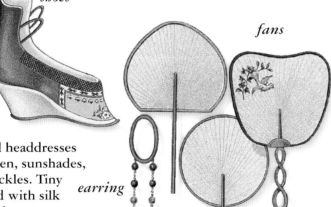

fans

earring

The first Chinese fans were made of feathers or of silk stretched over a flat frame. In about A.D. 1000 folding fans came to China, probably from Japan. Chinese fans were then exported to Europe.

4 Using scissors, cut each balsa strip ½ in. narrower (¼ in. each side) for half of its length. Make a compass hole at the base of each strip.

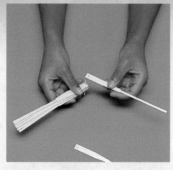

5 Stack strips. Pass a wooden skewer through holes. It must be long enough to fit through and overlap either side. Make sure strips can move freely.

6 Fold the paper backward and forward to form an accordian. Glue each alternate fold of the paper to the narrow ends of the strips, as shown.

7 Paint top strip of fan pink. Let dry. Cut out small cardboard discs. Glue them over the ends of the wooden skewer to secure the strips. Now cool off!

Chinese Art

IN IMPERIAL CHINA, painting was believed to be the finest of all the arts. It was considered to be a mark of civilization and a suitable pastime for scholars and even emperors. Painting was based upon the same ideas of harmony and simplicity that were important in the Daoist and Buddhist faiths. Paintings appeared on scrolls of silk and paper, walls, screens and fans. Popular subjects for pictures varied over the ages. They included the misty mountains and rivers of southern China, as well as landscapes set off by lone human figures. Artists also painted birds, animals and plants, such as bamboo or lotus. Sometimes just a few brush strokes were used to capture the spirit of the subject. Chinese writing in the form of a poem often played an important part in many pictures. Chinese artists also produced woodcuts, which are prints made from a carved wooden block. Traditionally these were not valued as much as the paintings, but many beautiful woodcuts were produced during the reign of the Ming dynasty (1368–1644).

SYMBOLS OF WISDOM
To the Chinese, the dragon embodied wisdom, strength and goodness. This intricate ivory seal belonged to a Ming emperor and shows a dragon guarding the pearl of wisdom.

WINDOW ON THE PAST
A royal procession makes its way along a mountain range. This detail from a painting on silk is by the great master Li Sixun (A.D. 651–716). Many Tang dynasty paintings show court life and royal processions, but they are far from dull. They provide a colorful glimpse of life in China at that time. This picture shows what people wore and how they traveled.

MAKE PAPER CUT-OUTS
You will need: colored paper, pencil, ruler, scissors.

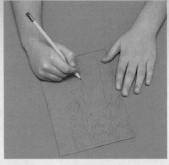

1 Take a piece of colored paper and lay it flat on a hard surface. Fold it exactly in half horizontally. Make a firm crease along the fold, as shown above.

2 Draw a Chinese-style design on the paper. Make sure all the shapes meet up at the fold. Make a tracing of your design so you can use it again.

3 Keeping the paper folded, cut out shapes. Make sure you don't cut along the folded edge. Cut away areas you want to discard in between shapes.

AT FULL GALLOP

Chinese artists greatly admired horses and loved to try to capture their strength and movement in paintings. This lively wall painting was found in a Han dynasty tomb.

PAINTING NATURE

Morning mist hangs over a mountain backdop. This detail from a masterpiece by Qiu Ying (1494–1552) was inspired by the forests and mountain landscapes of his homeland. Artists such as Qiu Ying were successful and well paid.

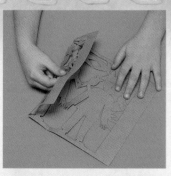

ART IN PORCELAIN

China's craft workers and designers were also great artists. This blue-and-white porcelain wine jar was made in the 1600s in the form of a mandarin duck and drake. Its hand-painted details would have taken many long hours of work to complete. Blue-and-white porcelain was very popular during the Ming dynasty.

SPRINGTIME ON PAPER

A watercolor painting from the 1800s shows a peach tree just as it comes into flower. It is painted in a very realistic, delicate and simple style. This approach is a common characteristic of much Chinese art.

4 Now open up your design. Be careful not to tear it. To add details to the figures, fold paper again. Mark the details to be cut along the crease.

5 Using a pair of scissors, carefully cut out the detail along the crease. The cut-out detail will be matched perfectly on the other side of the figure.

Open up your finished cut-out. Display by sticking it to a window, so that light shines through. Ask an adult for permission first. In China, paper cut-outs are used to bring good luck.

The Written Word

THE CHINESE LANGUAGE is written down with symbols called characters, which stand for sounds and words. They have changed and developed over the ages. A dictionary published in 1716 lists over 40,000 of them. Each character was painted by hand with a brush, using 11 basic brush strokes. The painting of these beautiful characters is called calligraphy, and was always seen as a form of art.

The Chinese began using woodblocks for printing about 1600 B.C. Before that, books had often been handwritten on bamboo strips. Ancient Chinese writers produced all sorts of practical handbooks and encyclopedias. Poetry first developed about 3,000 years ago. It was the Chinese who invented paper, nearly 2,000 years ago. Cloth or bark was shredded, pulped and dried on frames. Movable type was invented in the 1040s. In the 1500s popular folk tales such as *The Water Margin* were published, and in the 1700s the writer Cao Xuequin produced China's greatest novel, *A Dream of Red Mansions.*

MAGICAL MESSAGES
The earliest surviving Chinese script appears on animal bones. They were used for telling fortunes in about 1200 B.C. The script was made up of small pictures representing objects or ideas. Modern Chinese script is made up of patterns of lines.

ART OF CALLIGRAPHY
This text was handwritten during the Tang dynasty (A.D. 618–906). Traditional Chinese writing reads down from right to left, starting in the top right-hand corner.

MAKE PRINTING BLOCKS

You will need: plain white paper, pencil, paint, soft Chinese brush or thin paintbrush, water container, tracing paper, board, self-drying clay (6 in x 8 in, 1 in thick), modeling tool, wood glue, block printing ink, damp rag.

1 Copy or trace the characters from the reversed image block (see opposite). Start off with a pencil outline, then fill in with paint. Let dry.

2 Copy design onto tracing paper. Turn the paper over. Place it on the clay. Scribble on the clean side of the paper to leave a mirror image in the clay.

3 Use a modeling tool to carve out characters. Cut away clay all around characters to make a relief (raised pattern). Smooth clay base with your fingertips.

THE BEST WAY TO WRITE

A calligrapher of the 1840s begins to write, surrounded by his assistants. The brush must be held upright for the writing of Chinese characters. The wrist is never rested on the table. Many years of practice and study are necessary to become a good calligrapher.

INKS AND COLORS

Watercolors and inks were based on plant and mineral pigments in reds, browns, blues, greens and yellows. Black ink was made from carbon, obtained from soot. This was mixed with glue to form a solid block. The ink block would be wetted during use. Brushes were made from animal hair fitted into bamboo handles.

Chinese brushes

THE PRINTED PAGE

The Buddhist scripture called the Diamond Sutra *(shown right)* is probably the oldest surviving printed book in the world. It includes both text and pictures. The book was printed from a woodblock on May 11, A.D. 868 and was intended to be distributed at no cost to the public.

reversed image   *actual image*

Block rubbings of characters were an early form of printing.

Moon   Ruler

Mouth   Sun

4 When the relief has dried, paint the clay block with wood glue. Let dry thoroughly. When dry, the glue seals and protects the pattern.

5 Now paint the design. Apply a thick layer of printing ink to the raised parts of the clay with a Chinese brush or a soft paintbrush.

6 Lay a thin piece of plain white paper over the inked block. Use a dry brush to press the paper into the ink, so that the paper takes up the design.

7 Lift up the paper to reveal your design. Take care of your printing block by cleaning it with a damp rag. You can then use it again and again.

Musicians and Performers

THE EARLIEST CHINESE POETRY was sung rather than spoken. *Shijing* (the Book of Songs) dates back over 3,000 years and includes the words to hymns and folk songs. For most of China's history, musicians were employed in wealthy households. Orchestras played drums, gongs, pan pipes, racks of bronze bells, fiddles and other stringed instruments. Music was considered an important part of life, and models of musicians were often put in tombs to provide entertainment in the afterlife.

Musicians were frequently accompanied by acrobats, jugglers and magicians. Such acts were as popular in the markets and streets of the town as in the courtyards of nobles. Storytelling and puppet shows were equally well loved. Plays and opera became hugely popular in the A.D. 1200s, with tales of murder, intrigue, heroism and love acted out to music. Most of the female roles would be played by men.

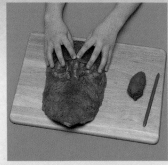

THE COURT DANCER
Arching her right arm upward, an elegant dancer performs at the royal court. The model's flowing dress belongs to the fashions of the Tang dynasty (A.D. 618–906).

PUTTING ON A PUPPET SHOW
Children put on a show with marionettes (puppets moved by strings) in the 1600s. Drumming was used to provide musical accompaniment, just like in a professional play of the period.

MAKE A MASK

You will need: tape measure, large block of self-drying clay, board, modeling tool, petroleum jelly, newspaper, wood glue and brush, scissors, thick cardboard, masking tape, 2 large white beads, paintbrush, paints (gray, cream, terra-cotta and yellow), water container, needle, black yarn, string.

1 Measure the width and length of your face with a tape measure. Make a clay mold. Carve out the eyes and attach a clay nose to the mask.

2 Paint front of mask with petroleum jelly. Apply 4–6 layers of papier-mâché. This is made by soaking torn newspaper in water and glue. Let dry.

3 Remove mask from the clay mold. Cut a 1 in. wide strip of cardboard long enough to fit around your face. Bend it into a circle, and tape to the mask.

50

MUSIC IN THE GARDEN

Musicians in the 1800s play *qins* (lutes) and *sheng* (flutes) in a garden setting. The music tried to reflect nature's harmony. It was intended to make the listener feel peaceful and spiritual.

CHINESE OPERA

These stars of the Chinese opera are performing in the 1700s. Well-known folk tales were acted out to the dramatic sound of crashing cymbals and high-pitched singing. Elaborate make-up and fancy costumes made it clear to the audience whether the actor was playing a hero or a villain, a princess or a demon.

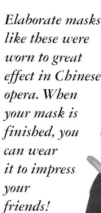

Elaborate masks like these were worn to great effect in Chinese opera. When your mask is finished, you can wear it to impress your friends!

SOUND THE DRUMS!

The cavalcade that followed an important government official or general might have included mounted drummers or trumpeters. These figures of musicians on horseback were found in the tomb of a high-ranking official from the Tang dynasty.

4 Cut 2 pointed ear shapes from cardboard. Fold cardboard at the edge to make flaps. Cut out and glue on small, decorative pieces of cardboard. Glue ears to the mask.

5 Glue on 2 large white beads for the eyes. Cut out more small pieces of cardboard. Glue these on above the eyes. Add another piece of cardboard for the lips.

6 Paint the mask with the gray base color first. Let dry. Then add details using the brighter colors. When dry, varnish with wood glue.

7 Use a needle to thread black yarn through for the beard. Tape yarn to back of the mask. Thread string through sides to hold mask on your face.

Games and Pastimes

Ｆrom early in China's history, kings and nobles loved to go hunting for pleasure. Horses and chariots were used to hunt deer and wild boar. Dogs and even cheetahs were trained to chase the prey. Spears, bows and arrows were then used to kill it. Falconry (using birds of prey to hunt animals) was commonplace by about 2000 B.C..

In the Ming and Qing dynasties ancient spiritual disciplines used by Daoist monks were brought together with the battle training used by warriors. These martial arts (*wu shu*) were intended to train both mind and body. They came to include the body movements known as tai chi (*taijiquan*), sword play (*jianwu*) and the extreme combat known as kung fu (*gongfu*).

Archery was a popular sport in imperial China. The Chinese also loved gambling, and may have invented the first card games over 2,000 years ago.

PEACE THROUGH MOVEMENT
A student of tai chi practices his art. The Chinese first developed the system of exercises known as tai chi more than 2,000 years ago. The techniques of tai chi were designed to help relax the human body and concentrate the mind.

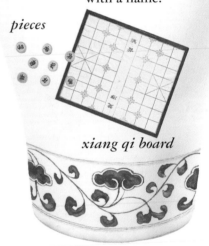

CHINESE CHESS
The traditional Chinese game of xiang qi is similar to western chess. One army battles against another, with round discs used as playing pieces. To tell the discs apart, each is marked with a name.

pieces

xiang qi board

MAKE A KITE

You will need: 11 in wooden skewers (x12), ruler, scissors, glue and brush, plastic insulating tape, paper, pencil, paint (blue, red, yellow, black and pink), paintbrush, water container, string, piece of wooden dowel, small metal ring.

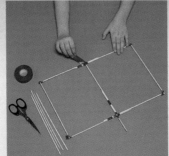

1 Make a 15¾ in x 11¾ in rectangle by joining some of the sticks. Overlap the sticks for strength, then glue and tape together. Add a centre rod.

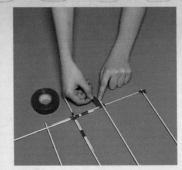

2 Make another rectangle 6 in x 15¾ in long. Overlay the second rectangle on top of the first one. Tape rectangles together, as shown above.

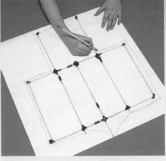

3 Place frame onto a sheet of white paper. Draw a 1 in border around outside of frame. Add curves around the end of the center rod.

BAMBOO BETTING
Gamblers place bets in a game of *liu po*. Bamboo sticks were thrown like dice to decide how far the markers on the board should move. Gambling was a widespread pastime during the Han dynasty. People would bet large sums of money on the outcomes of card games, horse races and cock fights.

POLO PONIES
These women from the Tang dynasty are playing a fast and furious game of polo. They are probably noblewomen from the emperor's royal court. The sport of polo was originally played in India and central Asia. It was invented as a training game to improve the riding skills of soldiers in cavalry units.

ALL-IN WRESTLING
This bronze figure of two wrestling muscle men was made in about 300 B.C. Wrestling was a very popular form of entertainment and sport in imperial China. It continues to be an attraction at country fairs and festivals.

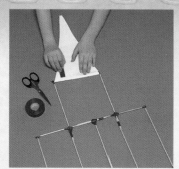

Chinese children today still play with homemade paper kites. Kites were invented in China in about 400 B.C.

4 Cut out the kite shape from the paper. Using a pencil, draw the details of your dragon design on the paper. Paint in your design and let dry.

5 Cut a triangular piece of paper to hang from the end of your kite as a tail. Fold tail over rod at bottom of kite, as shown. Tape tail into position.

6 Carefully tape and glue your design onto the frame. Fold over border that you allowed for when cutting out the paper. Tape to back of paper, as shown.

7 Wrap 30 ft. of string around dowel. Tie other end to ring. From the back, thread 2 pieces of string through kite. Tie ends to center rod. Tie other ends to ring.

Travel by Land

THE CHINESE EMPIRE was linked by a network of roads used only by the army, officials and royal messengers. A special carriageway was reserved for the emperor himself. Ordinary people traveled along dusty or muddy routes and tracks.

China's mountainous landscape and large number of rivers meant that Chinese engineers became expert at bridge-building. Suspension bridges made of rope and bamboo were being used from about A.D. 1 onward. A bridge suspended from iron chains crossed the Chang Jiang (Yangzi River) as early as A.D. 580. A stone arch bridge built in about A.D. 615 still stands today at Zhouxian in Hebei province. Most people traveled by foot, and porters often had to carry great loads on their backs. They also carried wealthy people from place to place on litters (chairs).

China's small native ponies were interbred with larger, stronger horses from central Asia sometime after 100 B.C. This provided fast, powerful mounts that were suitable for messengers and officials, and they were also capable of pulling chariots and carriages. Mules and camels were widely used along the trade routes of the north, while shaggy yaks carried loads in the high mountains of the Himalayas. Carts were usually hauled along by oxen.

HEADING OUT WEST
Chinese horsemen escort the camels of a caravan (trading expedition). The traders are about to set out along the Silk Road. This trading route ran all the way from Chang'an (Xian) in China right through to Europe and the lands of the Mediterranean.

RIDING ON HORSEBACK
A Chinese nobleman from about 2,000 years ago reins in his elegant horse. Breaking in the horse would have been difficult, as the rider has no stirrups and could easily be unseated. Metal stirrups were in general use in China by A.D. 302. They provided more stability and helped to improve the rider's control of the horse.

CAMEL POWER
Bactrian (two-humped) camels were originally bred in central Asia. They could endure the extremes of heat and cold of the region, and travel for long distances without water. This toughness made them ideal for transporting goods along the Silk Road.

CARRIED BY HAND
A wealthy landowner of the Qing dynasty travels around his estates. He is carried along in a litter, a platform supported by the shoulders of his tired servants. An umbrella shades the landowner from the heat of the summer sun.

HAN CARRIAGE
During the Han period, three-horse carriages were used by the imperial family only. This carving from a tomb brick is probably of a messenger carrying an important order from the emperor.

TRAVELING IN STYLE
During the Han dynasty, government officials traveled in stylish horse-drawn carriages. This picture is taken from a decorative brick found in a Han tomb. After larger, stronger breeds of horses were introduced into China from central Asia, the horse became a status symbol for the rich and powerful. Such horses were considered to be celestial (heavenly).

Junks and Sampans

Ｆ**ROM EARLY IN** Ｃ**HINA'S** history, its rivers, lakes and manmade canals were the country's main highways. Fishermen propelled small wooden boats across the water with a single oar or pole at the stern. These small boats were often roofed with mats, like the sampans (which means "three planks" in Chinese) still seen today. Large wooden sailing ships, which we call junks, sailed the open ocean. They were keeled (flat-bottomed) with a high stern and square bows. Their sails were made of matting stiffened with strips of bamboo. By the A.D. 800s, Chinese shipbuilders had built the first ships with several masts and proper rudders.

In the 1400s, admirals Zheng He and Wang Jinghong led seven sea expeditions that visited Southeast Asia, India, Arabia and East Africa. The flagship of their 300-strong naval fleet was over five times the size of the largest European ships of the time.

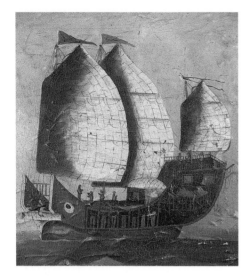

IN FULL SAIL
Junks were a type of sailing vessel used by merchants in the East and South China seas. They were also used by pirates. The China seas could be blue and peaceful, but they were often whipped into a fury by typhoons (tropical storms).

RIVER TRAFFIC
All sorts of small trading boats were sailed or rowed along China's rivers in the 1850s. River travel was often difficult and could be dangerous. Floods were common along the Huang He (Yellow River), which often changed course. The upper parts of China's longest river, the Chang Jiang (Yangzi River), were rocky and had powerful currents.

MAKE A SAMPAN

You will need: ruler, pencil, thick and thin cardboard, scissors, glue and brush, masking tape, 6 wooden skewers, string, thin yellow paper, paint (black, dark and brown), paintbrush, water container.

15½ in — Runner A (x2) — ½ in
13¼ in — Side B (x2) — 2 in — 6 in
Base C (x2) — 6 in — 2¾ in
Base D — 7 in
Floor E — 4 in — 2¾ in — 1½ in
Floor F (x2) — 2¾ in
Edge G (x2) — 2½ in — ½ in

Cut pieces B, C, D and G from thick cardboard. Cut pieces A, E, and F from thin cardboard.

1 Glue base pieces C and D to side B, as shown. Hold the pieces with masking tape while the glue dries. When dry, remove the masking tape.

2 Glue remaining side B to the boat. Stick runner A pieces to top of the sides. Make sure the ends jut out 1 in. at the front and back of the boat.

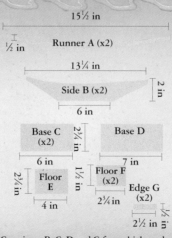

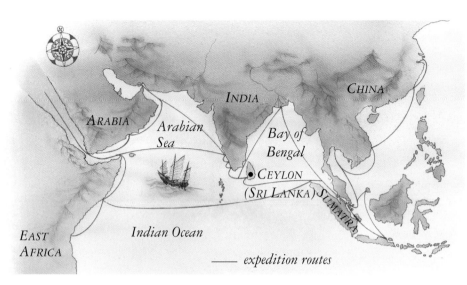

FISHERMEN'S FEASTS

Seas, lakes and rivers were an important food source in imperial China. Drying fish was often the only way to preserve it in the days before refrigeration. Dried fish made strong-tasting sauces and soups. Popular seafoods included crabs, shrimp and squid.

dried fish

dried squid

THE VOYAGES OF ZHENG HE

Chinese admirals Zheng He and Wang Jinghong carried out seven fantastic voyages of exploration between 1405 and 1433. This map shows how far and wide they traveled on these expeditions. Their impressive fleets included over 60 ships crewed by about 27,000 seamen, officers and interpreters. The biggest of their vessels was 482 feet long and 197 feet wide.

THE FISHING TRIP

A fisherman poles his boat across the river in the 1500s. The bird shown in the picture is a tamed cormorant, used for catching the fish. The cormorant was normally attached to a line, with a ring around its neck to prevent it from swallowing the fish.

To add the finishing touch to your sampan, make a boatman and oar to propel the vessel through the waterways.

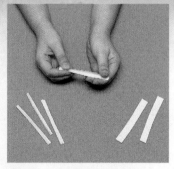

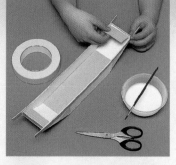

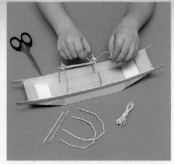

3 Glue floor E to center of base. Add floor F pieces to the ends of the base, as shown. Stick edge G pieces in between the ends of the runners.

4 Bend 2 wooden skewers into 4 in. high arches. Cut 2 more sticks into five 4 in. struts. Glue and tie 2 struts to the sides of the arches and 1 to the top.

5 Repeat step 4 to make a second roof. To make roof matting, cut thin yellow paper into ½ in. x 4 in. wide strips. Fold the strips in half and stitch.

6 Paint boat and roofs brown. Let dry. Glue the matting strips to the roofs, as shown. When the glue is dry, place roofs inside the boat.

Soldiers and Weapons

IN CHINA'S EARLY HISTORY, bitter warfare between local rulers devastated the countryside with an appalling cost in human lives. Battle tactics and campaigns were discussed in *The Art of War* by Sun-Tzu, who lived in the 500s B.C. at around the same time as the thinker Kong Fuzi (Confucius). This was the first book of its kind, and its ideas are still studied today. After the empire was united in 221 B.C., rulers still needed large armies to stay in power and to guard against invasion.

The first Chinese armies fought with horse-drawn chariots and bronze weapons. Later, battles were fought with iron weapons, horsemen and hundreds of thousands of conscripted footsoldiers. Armor was made of metal, lacquered leather or padded quilting. Weapons included bows and arrows, powerful crossbows, swords and halberds (long blades on poles). As China's empire grew, there were armed conflicts with peoples whose lands had been conquered.

PRECIOUS SPEAR
This spearhead is over 3,200 years old. It was made from the precious stone jade set in bronze and turquoise. The spear was intended for ceremonial use, as it was far too precious to be used in combat.

SOLDIER ON HORSEBACK
A Tang dynasty warrior sits astride his horse, ready for battle. His horse is also ready to fight, covered by a protective jacket. The warrior's feet are supported by stirrups. These were useful in combat, as they allowed a soldier to remain steady in the saddle as he fought.

MAKE ARMOR

You will need: 5 ft. x 2¼ ft. felt fabric, scissors, large sewing needle, string, silver card stock, ruler, pencil, tape, paper fasteners, silver paint, paintbrush, water container, thick cardboard, glue and brush.

1 Fold felt fabric in half. Cut a semicircle along fold to make a neck hole. Put garment on. Trim so it just reaches your hips and covers your shoulders.

2 Use scissors to make 2 holes either side of the waist. Pass string through holes. Secure as shown. The string will be used to tie the garment around your waist.

3 Cut 70 squares (2 in. x 2 in.) out of silver card stock. Lay a row of overlapping squares face down at the top of the fabric. Tape the rows together.

FIGHTING ON THE GREAT WALL

In 1884–1885, heavily armed French soldiers battled with the Chinese. The empire was in decline by the 1880s, and its outdated tactics were no match for the superior might of the French forces.

BATTLING HAN

This battered-looking helmet would once have protected a Han soldier's head from crossbow bolts, sword blows and arrows. Young men were conscripted into the Chinese army and had to serve as soldiers for at least two years. During this time they received no payment. However, they were supplied with food, weapons and armor.

FRONTIER GUARD

A battle-hardened soldier keeps guard with his shield and spear. A warrior like this would have kept watch over the precious Silk Road in a distant outpost of the Chinese empire. This model dates from the reign of the Tang Emperor Taizong (A.D. 626–649).

To put on your armor, pull the undergarment over your head. Ask a friend to help with the waist ties. Make holes in the shoulder pads and tie on with string.

4 Make enough rows to cover fabric. Trim card stock to fit at neck. Tape rows together. Turn armor over. Attach paper fasteners at corners.

5 Place armor over fabric. Push paper fasteners through top and bottom corners of armor. Pass fasteners through fabric and fasten. Paint fasteners silver.

6 Cut shoulder pads out of thick cardboard. Cut out 2 in. squares of silver card stock to cover pads. Glue to cardboard. Push fasteners through. Paint fasteners silver.

Festivals and Customs

THE CHINESE FESTIVAL best known around the world today is the New Year or Spring Festival. Its date varies according to the traditional Chinese calendar, which is based on the phases of the moon. The festival is marked by dancers carrying a lone dragon through the streets, accompanied by loud, crackling firecrackers to scare away evil spirits. The festival has been celebrated for over 2,000 years and has always been a time for family feasts and village carnivals. The doorways of buildings are traditionally decorated with hand-written poetry on strips of red paper to bring luck and good fortune for the coming year.

Soon after New Year, sweet dumplings made of rice flour are prepared for the Lantern Festival. Paper lanterns are hung out to mirror the first full moon of the year. This festival began during the Tang dynasty (A.D. 618–906). In the eighth month of the year, the autumn full moon is marked by the eating of special moon cakes. Many Chinese festivals are linked to a region or people. These include celebrations of sowing and harvest, dances, horse races and the eating of specially prepared foods.

DANCING ANIMALS
Chinese New Year parades are often headed by a lion (*shown above*) or dragon. These are carried by dancers accompanied by crashing cymbals. The first month of the Chinese calendar begins on the first full moon between January 21st and February 19th.

HORSE RACING
The Mongols, who invaded China in the 1200s, brought with them their love of horses and superb riding skills. Today, children as young as three years old take part in horse-racing festivals in northern China and Mongolia. Archery and wrestling competitions are also regularly held.

MAKE A LANTERN

You will need: thick cardboard, pencil, ruler, scissors, compass, glue and brush, red tissue paper, blue paint, paintbrush, water container, thin blue and yellow card stock, wire, tape, bamboo stick, flashlight, fringing fabric.

Frame (x4) — 10 in, 2¼ in
Side (x4) — ½ in, 1 in, 6¼ in
End (x2) — 7 in, 7 in

Using the measurements above, draw the 10 pieces on the thick card stock (pieces not drawn to scale). Cut out pieces.

1 Using compass, draw a 3 in diameter circle in the middle of one of the end pieces. Cut out the circle with scissors. Glue on the 4 sides, as shown.

2 Glue together the frame pieces. Then glue the end pieces onto the frame. When dry, cover frame with red tissue paper. Glue one side at a time.

DRAGON BOATS

In the fifth month of the Chinese year, races are held in the Dragon Boat festival. This is in memory of a famous statesman named Qu Yuan, who drowned himself in 278 B.C. when his advice to his ruler was ignored. Rice dumplings are eaten at the Dragon Boat festival every year in his memory.

CHINESE LANTERNS

Elaborate paper lanterns brighten up a wedding in the 1800s during the Qing dynasty. Lanterns were also strung up or paraded on poles at other private celebrations and during Chinese festivals.

3 Paint top of lantern blue. Cut borders out of blue card stock. Glue to top and bottom of frame. Stick a thin strip of yellow card stock to bottom border.

4 Make 2 small holes opposite each other at top of lantern. Pass the ends of a loop of wire through each hole. Bend and tape ends to secure wire.

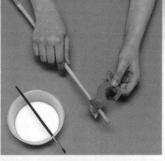

5 Make a hook from thick cardboard. Split end opposite hook. Glue and wrap around bamboo stick. Hang lantern by wire loop from hook.

Light up your lantern by placing a small flashlight inside it. Decorate with a fringe. Now you can join in Chinese celebrations!

61

Glossary

A

abacus A wooden frame with beads on rods, used for calculating.

acupuncture The treatment of the body with fine needles for the relief of pain or to cure illness.

alloy A substance made by mixing two or more different metals.

ancestor An individual from whom one is descended, such as a great, great-grandfather.

Anno Domini (A.D.) A system used to calculate dates after the supposed year of Christ's birth. Anno Domini dates in this book are prefixed A.D. up to the year 1000 (e.g. A.D. 521). After 1000, no prefixes are used (e.g. 1912).

archaeologist A person who studies ancient ruins and remains.

astronomy The scientific study of stars, planets and other heavenly bodies. In ancient times it was often mixed up with astrology, the belief that heavenly bodies shape our lives.

B

banquet A rich, elaborate feast served with great ceremony.

barter To trade by exchanging goods rather than by paying money.

Before Christ (B.C.) A system used to calculate dates before the supposed year of Christ's birth. Dates are calculated in reverse (e.g. 200 B.C. is longer ago than 1 B.C.). Before Christ dates are followed by the letters B.C. (e.g. 455 B.C.).

bellows A mechanism for pumping air into a fire or furnace.

Buddhism The religious teachings of the Buddha. Buddhism first came to China from India.

C

character One of the symbols used in Chinese script.

civilization A society that makes advances in law, government, the arts and technology.

civil servant Official who carries out government administration.

Confucianism The Western name for the teachings of the philosopher Kong Fuzi (Confucius), which call for social order and respect for one's family and ancestors.

cormorant A coastal and river bird that can be trained to catch fish.

crossbow A mechanical bow that fires small arrows called bolts.

D

Daoism A Chinese philosophy based on contemplation of the natural world. It later became a religion with a belief in magic.

derrick The tower-like frame that supports drilling equipment.

dynasty A period of rule by emperors of the same royal family. The most important dynasties in the history of the Chinese empire are listed below:

Xia (c.2100 B.C.–c.1600 B.C.)

Shang (c.1600 B.C.–1122 B.C.)

Zhou (1122 B.C.–221 B.C.)

　Western Zhou (1122 B.C.-771 B.C.)

　Eastern Zhou (771 B.C.–221 B.C.)

Qin (221 B.C.–206 B.C.)

Han (206 B.C.–A.D. 220)

Three Kingdoms Period
　(A.D. 220–280)

Jin (A.D. 265–420)

Northern and Southern
　Dynasties (A.D. 420–581)

Sui (A.D. 581–618)

Tang (A.D. 618–906)

Five Kingdoms and Ten Dynasties
　Period (A.D. 906-960)

Song (960–1279)

Yuan (1279–1368)

Ming (1368–1644)

Qing (1644–1912)

E

escapement A type of ratchet used in clockwork timing mechanisms.

F

filament A fine strand of fiber.

Forbidden City The royal palace in Beijing, made up of hundreds of buildings set inside high walls.

H

harmony A pleasing sense of order, based on peace and balance.

hemp A fibrous plant, often used to make coarse textiles and clothes.

I

imperial Relating to the rule of an emperor or empress.

Islam The Muslim faith, which proclaims that there is only one God and that his messenger is the prophet Muhammad.

J

jade Either of two precious, hard minerals called jadeite and nephrite. Jade is white or green in color.

joinery Skilled woodworking needed for making fine furniture.

junk A traditional flat-bottomed Chinese sailing ship with square sails.

K

kaolin A fine white clay used in porcelain and paper making.

kitchen god A god whose picture was kept in Chinese kitchens.

L

lacquer A thick, colored varnish used to coat wood, metal or leather.

lodestone A type of magnetic iron ore, also called magnetite.

loom A frame or machine used for weaving cloth.

lotus A type of water lily.

lychee A soft Chinese fruit.

M

magistrate An imperial officer of justice, similar to a local judge.

martial arts Physical exercises that are often based upon combat, such as swordplay and kung fu. Chinese martial arts bring together spiritual and physical disciplines.

merchant A person who buys and sells goods for a profit.

millet A type of grain crop.

mint The process by which new coins are produced.

mother-of-pearl A hard, shiny substance found in shells, also known as nacre. It was often used in jewelry inlays by skilled Chinese craft workers.

moxibustion The transfer of heat to the body from burning herbs.

mung beans The seeds of the Asian mung plant. Often used as a source of bean sprouts.

myth Any ancient tale or legend that describes gods, spirits or fantastic creatures.

P

pagoda A high, multi-story tower found in eastern and southern Asia. Pagodas were often used as libraries or places of religious worship.

peasant A poor country dweller.

pigment Any material used to provide color for paint or ink.

pinyin The official romanized spelling of the Chinese language, used for terms and place names in this book. In pinyin, the letter q is pronounced *ch*.

porcelain The finest quality of pottery. It was made with kaolin and baked at a high temperature.

province Part of the empire marked off for administrative purposes.

R

ritual An often repeated series of solemn actions, normally carried out for a religious purpose.

S

sampan A small wooden boat with a cabin made of matting.

seismoscope An instrument that reacts to earthquakes and tremors.

sericulture The production of silk.

Silk Road The overland trading route that, in ancient times, stretched from northern China through Asia to Europe.

silkworm The larva (caterpillar) of a silkmoth. It produces silken threads that it spins into a cocoon.

smelt To extract a metal from its ore by heating it in a furnace.

suspension bridge A bridge in which the roadway is suspended (hung) from towers.

T

temple A building used for worship or rituals. Such buildings were often specially designed for this purpose.

terra-cotta A composition of baked clay and sand used to make statues, figurines and pottery.

textile Any cloth that has been woven, such as silk or cotton.

threshing To beat or thrash out grain from the corn.

tomb A vault in which dead bodies are placed. In imperial China, the tombs of emperors and noblemen were often filled with beautiful objects of great value.

W

ward A walled district found in the cities of imperial China.

warlord A man who keeps a private army and controls a large region of the country by force.

winnow To sift the grain from the chaff (husks) of the corn.

wisteria A Chinese climbing shrub with blue flowers.

X

xianq qi A traditional Chinese board game, similar to the Western game of chess.

Y

yak A long-haired ox, used in Tibet as a beast of burden.

yin and yang The Daoist belief in two life forces that must be balanced to achieve harmony. Ying is negative, feminine and dark, while yang is posirive, masculine and light.

Index

A

abacus 30-1
acupuncture 30
armor 58-9
astronomy 30, 35

B

bamboo 18, 20, 21, 26, 46, 48, 53, 54, 56
Beijing 5, 8, 9, 10, 11, 16, 32, 38, 39
Boxer Rebellion 9
bronze 4, 20, 21, 27, 38-9, 44
Buddhism 6, 7, 12-13, 16-17, 36, 37, 38, 46, 49

C

calendar 6, 60
calligraphy 48-9
Chang'an (Xian) 4, 5, 13, 17, 28, 29, 54
Chang Jiang (Yangzi River) 6, 7, 54, 56
Christianity 12
civil service 14, 15, 22, 45
Confucianism 5, 8, 12, 22

D

Daoism 5, 6, 8, 12, 30, 46, 52
dragons 19, 38, 43, 44, 46, 60
dynasties 10, 62

E

earthquakes 34, 35
education 14, 15, 22
emperors 4, 8-11, 44
engineering 32-3, 54
examinations 14, 15
exploration 8-9, 56-7

F

family life 22-3
farming 4, 14, 15, 24-5, 27
festivals 60-1
fingernails 39, 44
foot binding 22
Forbidden City 10, 11, 38, 39

G

gambling 52-3
games and pastimes 52-3
gardens 18-19, 21
Genghis Khan 8
Grand Canal 5, 6, 7, 8, 32-3
Great Wall 5, 6, 7, 32-3, 59
Guangzhou (Canton) 17
gunpowder 34

H

Han dynasty 5, 6, 9, 18, 22, 36, 62
Han Gaozu (Liu Bang) 5, 9
Hong Kong 9
horses 47, 53, 54-5, 58, 60
Huang He (Yellow River) 6, 7, 56
hunting 4, 52

I

inventions 15, 24, 28, 30-1, 34-5
iron 5, 24, 38-9, 54
Islam 7, 12, 13

J

jade 5, 20, 36-7, 44, 58
jewelry 38-9, 44-45
junks 56-7

K

Kaifeng 29
kites 52-53
Kong Fuzi (Confucius) 5, 8, 12, 14, 15, 22, 58
Kublai Khan 8, 9
kung fu 52

L

lacquer 40-1, 58
lamps and lanterns 20, 60-1
Laozi 5, 8
Li Bai 7
Li Sixun 46
litters 11, 54, 55
Liu Sheng 5, 20, 36
Liu Xiu 6
Li Zicheng 9
locks and keys 34
Longshan culture 4

M

Manchus 6, 9, 44
martial arts 52
medicine 30-1
merchants 14, 15, 28-9, 40, 44
metal working 4, 5, 38-9
Ming dynasty 6, 7, 8, 9, 36, 41, 46, 47, 52, 62
mining 32
money 8, 15, 28
Mongols 6, 8-9, 32, 60
music and dance 50-1

N

Nanjing, Treaty of 9
New Year 26, 29, 60

O

Opium Wars 9

P

pagodas 16-17
painting 21, 22, 46-7
palaces 4, 10, 11, 16, 21
peasants 14-15, 33
peoples 6
pigtails 44
plays and operas 50-1
poetry 6, 7, 48, 50
Polo, Marco 8, 9, 33
porcelain 20, 28, 40-1, 47
pottery 4, 15, 24, 40-1
printing 7, 8, 34-5, 46, 48-9
puppets 50
Puyi 9

Q

Qin dynasty 9, 62
Qing dynasty 9, 10, 11, 15, 41, 44, 52, 62
Qin Shi Huangdi (Zheng) 4, 5, 9, 11, 28

R

religion 5, 6, 7, 8, 10, 12-13, 26
Red Turban Rebellion 8
Republic of China 6, 9
rice 15, 24-7

S

sampans 56-7
science 30-1, 34-5
Shang dynasty 4, 10, 16, 26, 27, 38, 62
ships 34, 42, 56-7
silk 4, 15, 20, 28, 34, 42-3, 44, 45, 46
Silk Road 5, 7, 28-9, 54-5, 59
smelting 38-9
Song dynasty 8, 22, 29, 62
Stone Age 4, 36
Sui dynasty 6, 32, 62

T

tai chi 52
Tang dynasty 6, 20, 24, 26, 28, 29, 45, 46, 58, 62
tea 15, 24, 28
temples 4, 5, 7, 10, 13, 16, 19
terra-cotta army 4, 5
Tibet and Tibetans 6, 11, 17
tombs 4, 5, 20, 36-7, 41, 47
tools 15, 24, 37, 38
trade 5, 6, 7, 14, 15, 17, 28-9, 40, 41, 54-7
transport 11, 32-3, 42, 54-7

W

weapons 37, 38, 52, 58-9
weddings 22, 61
Western powers 9, 11, 17, 59
women 8-9, 22-3, 26, 42, 45, 53
writing 22, 48-9
Wu Zetian 7, 9, 39

X

Xia dynasty 4, 10, 62

Y

Yangshao culture 4
Yellow Turban Rebellion 6
yin and yang 12
Yuan dynasty 8

Z

Zhang Heng 34, 35
Zheng He 8-9, 56-7
Zhou dynasty 4, 5, 10